SOUTH OF THE SUNSET

Voyage to Anguar
and other World War II Poems
of the South Pacific

By Earl Victor Shaffer

Veteran of Army Signal Corp Service Battalion 572
stationed at Oahu, Hawaii 1942-1945

Published by

The Earl Shaffer Foundation, Inc.

www.earlshaffer.org

1948 boots

OTHER PUBLICATIONS OF THE EARL SHAFFER FOUNDATION

Walking With Spring, DVD slide show of Earl's 1948 hike

Always In April, an original folk music CD by Earl Shaffer

Trail Of The Tropic Moon, an original folk music CD by Earl

Songs of the Blue Ridge Runner, performed by Takoma Tedd

The Appalachian Trail: **Calling Me Back To The Hills**
  Large format book about Earl's 1998 hike
  Beautifully illustrated with photos by Bart Smith

Ode To The Appalachian Trail
  Earl's long lyrical poem chronicling his 1998 hike

Before I walked With Spring
  Earl's first book of World War II poems

Also by Earl Shaffer: ***Walking With Spring***, the story of Earl's 1948 hike, published by The Appalachian Trail Conservancy.

SOUTH OF THE SUNSET
Copyright 2011 The Earl Shaffer Foundation, Inc.
A 501c3 corporation **All Rights Reserved**

International Standard Book Number: 978-0-9795659-3-9

All materials and books available at www.earlshaffer.org
Poetry: Earl Victor Shaffer
Photos: Earl Victor Shaffer unless otherwise noted
Editor: Nancy Shaffer Nafziger
Production: John Shaffer
Pacific Map: Sanne Larsen Bagby and David Shaffer
Cover Design: David Shaffer
Cover Photos: From the Earl Shaffer Army collection.

DEDICATED to America's
MILITARY VETERANS
Who served to preserve our
American Ideals and Freedoms

THE GREATEST ARE NEVER KNOWN

In the maelstrom of life as it ebbs and flows
In its devious myriad trends,
The flower of manhood develops and grows
Midst the peril its growth transcends.

The choicest are not found on pedestals high
But out in the midst of the throng,
Doing their bit without murmur or sigh
Out where they think they belong.

And the greatest of all are the ones who know
That no one will know the deed;
Who know that too often fame crumbles to show
An empty and hollow creed.

There are those deserving a hero's name
That the eyes of men condone.
There are many who dwell in the Hall of Fame,
But the greatest are never known.

UNSUNG

Unscribbled in the annals of warfare
Are heroes boldly acclaimed--
Unknown through the records engraved there,
Unrecognized and unnamed.
The banners forgotten remain unsung
And many tales that lie

For manifold reasons as yet unsung
Nor bared to the public eye.
The far-reaching future becomes today.
And out of the winnowed scorn,
The dross and ill-deserved are shorn away
And lasting legend is born.
But round and about us may still be found
True tales that avoid the pen,
Too glaring with truth or as yet unbound
To the fettered words of men.

Earl with his guitar singing his original folk songs

FOREWARD

At a gathering of long distance hikers in Pennsylvania in 1998, shortly after completion of the 50th Anniversary thru-hike of his historic '48 thru-hike and at the age of 79, Earl Shaffer was questioned by a young hiker, "What accomplishment in your life are you most proud of?"

The answer was most surprising to all the hiking *aficionados* present that day since it came from one of the world's most famous hikers. In his barely audible voice, Earl Shaffer responded, "My military service."

As a young girl, I had heard that Uncle Earl had war poetry that he wanted to publish, but there seemed to be no one interested in World War II poetry during those early years after the war. Those hidden years on South Pacific atolls have now surfaced with this publication of the "South of the Sunset" poems and the previously published volume, **Before I Walked With Spring,** which chronicled his entire military service in poetic ballad form.

Uncle Earl released his tensions in the war zone by utilizing his amazing command of English rhetoric to vividly portray the people, places, machines, and military maneuvers in the Pacific War Theater, an area that he christened "South of the Sunset." He experimented with different forms of poetry, modeling his forms after those of Kipling, Tennyson, Byron, Whitman and others. Even the rare form of a heroic sonnet surfaced in this collection we've titled, **South of the Sunset**. "Battleships" contains the required extra quatrain and specified end rhyme scheme. However, Uncle Earl did stray from the usual meter and rhythm of a heroic sonnet.

In 1948, Earl Shaffer embarked on yet another "great adventure," as he described his plans to attempt a thru-hike of the entire Appalachian Trail. No such hike had ever been documented. First, he was endeavoring to fulfill a pact made before the war with Walter Winemiller, a close friend and Shiloh neighbor. They had planned to complete the thru-hike after their return from war. Other reasons to make the attempt at a thru-hike were to bring public attention to the Trail and, hopefully, create interest in his war poems. Along the over 2,000 miles, he journalized the trek in poetry and prose. After his prose account, **Walking With Spring**, had been rejected by a publishing company and then privately printed for family and friends, the Appalachian Trail Conservancy published his seminal work in 1983. Still, no one was interested in his war poetry.

Earl Shaffer became well known for his shelter building and indefatigable Trail maintenance and, eventually, completed two more thru-hikes of the Appalachian Trail: North to South in 1965 and South to North in 1998. He called the South to North hike in 1998, his "50th Anniversary Hike."

Both volumes of war poetry—***Before I Walked With Spring*** a**nd *South of the Sunset*—**complete a death bed promise made to Uncle Earl in 2002, as that was still his major concern. It also fulfills his promise to his World War II buddies. They considered the poetic war depictions so accurate that they had wanted the poetry published immediately. And now, those promises are fulfilled.
Nancy Shaffer Nafziger, editor

Nancy, on behalf of the Shaffer family, accepted Earl's award when he was inducted into the AT Museum Hall of Fame.
AT Museum photo

INTRODUCTION

As a boy I assumed that everyone had an Uncle Earl in the family, so he was not unusual to me. I gradually became aware of his unique qualities: sensitive nature, generosity, passionate about causes yet soft-spoken and of few words-—all attributes of a good poet.

When my brothers and I visited Aunt Anna's farm where Uncle Earl lived in his apartment above the barn, we usually hung out with Uncle Earl while he refinished and repaired antiques. We never felt unwelcome; he never told us to get lost. Sometimes he took us to auctions, on day hikes, and on trips to maintain the Appalachian Trail. Traveling in his "woody wagon" (wood paneled Dodge station wagon) and later in his VW vans was an experience. Usually we sat on wooden chairs because he had removed all passenger seats to maximize hauling space. Frequently, tools would fall out of holes in the floor as we traveled.

As young boys we admired the carefree life he represented. He was quite passionate about many subjects, as most acquaintances know, but he never directed that anger toward us. During that time, Uncle Earl rarely talked about himself or his accomplishments because he lived in the present. He would disappear for weeks hiking or doing Trail maintenance. After I married, he included Sarah in the family circle. The times in the twilight outside the barn talking and singing remain precious memories.

One time when I was with him, we stopped to visit an elderly family friend living in an old farmhouse heated by a fireplace. He left behind several bags of groceries and a warm feeling of friendship. I realized then that Uncle Earl had provided this man his place to live, applying the Biblical principle: "having compassion, making a difference" Jude 22. Uncle Earl was more than a conservationist—he was a minimalist. He lived, hiked, and camped frugally and light, applying the principles of Nessmuk, the pen name for George Washington Sears. Google him!

Uncle Earl never mowed more grass than necessary, never purchased a telephone, lived in a wood heated uninsulated space, and drove vehicles others would have abandoned. These attributes helped him to survive in the Pacific Theater of World War II.

His shorter poems show his minimalist ways and bring out his sensitive, passionate nature. Around a campfire he would be silent, listening to others, and obtain ideas for poetry. As a veteran of the Vietnam War, but having not experienced the extent of deprivation and isolation as Uncle Earl did, I can relate, in a small way, to his South Pacific poems. "Anguar Moon" and "To Understand" express well the loneliness of a soldier at war. Because he spent time around the campfires and in the mess halls and barracks with men of all service branches, he was able to apply the basic tenets of military life to all areas of service such as fighter pilots, gunners, sailors, and assault troops to name a few. The pathos in his poetry reveals a depth of understanding beyond the norm. Uncle Earl's Christian roots and personal faith show in many poems, especially "A Soldier's Creed," "Foxhole Prayer," and "To Anna."

Uncle Earl's life and poetry remind me of the famous quote: "War is days and weeks of boredom interrupted by moments of sheer terror," and his poetry shows both sides of that quote. He used the "days of boredom" writing poetry, giving future generations insight into events he prayed others would not have to endure. The "far-away look" in his eyes when he talked about the Appalachian Trail and the South Pacific showed where his passions lay.

What an honor it is to be asked to write an introduction to this collection of war poems by one of the most unique persons I have known.

Ray Shaffer, Cobra helicopter crew chief, Vietnam

CONTENTS

Author's Prayer
Map of World War II Pacific Theatre

Preface...**4**

Tell 'em Before the Dawn
To Understand
Lone Brave's Bondage
For Constancy

South of the Sunset................................**7 to 96**

Sullen Pacific
Radar Raconteurs
Radio # 6
To My Climbing Belt and Spurs
High Liner
Kaena High Line
Sweatshop of War
War Wanderers
Isle of Potte
Paradisiac
To Belep
Maitaki Land Boy
Long Range Bomber Crew
Nanumea Bound
Coral Sea Sortie
Negative Paradise
Never Ease
Battle Craze
Battle Graves
Niui Chrome
Nouvelle Caledonia, Adieu
Old Joe
Our Sacrifice
Battle Scar
Bigotry's Bale
Pacific Gripe
South Seas Glamour Tour
The Desert Isles
South of the Sunset
The Jeep
The Low Atolls
The Luck of the *Banshee's Wail*
The Movin' Picture Show

The Trail of Men Who Know
To Anna
Thinking of Home
Dunno
The Harvest of War
Thio Pass
Tide Lights
To a Foxhole
Foxhole Prayer
Nuisance Raid
To John Magee
To Mother Muldoon
Captain Wermuth
To Tex Davis
Tracer Song
Under One Moon
Atoll Evensong
Under The Shell
Utter Desecration
Vandal Moon
Warum?
Battleships
Who Judged the Tide?
Dirge of the Landing Barge
Advance Base
A Voice from Flanders
Chance Reunion
Dread Souvenir
Benevolent Castigation
Franklin Delano Roosevelt
Grave On Guadalcanal
Island War
Last Stop Interlude
Leaky Morale
Tarnished Brass
Men O' War
Ugly Ducklings
End of the Dawn Patrol
Queen of the Skies
Grumman Wildcat
Sometime the Dawn

World War II Journalists………………………….65 to 66
Sgt. Howard Brodie
Sgt. Mack Morris
To Ernie Pyle
Pacific Convoy…………………………………..66
Anguar Campaign……………………………67 to 96
To Dad If I Don't Come Home
A Soldier's Creed
Voyage To Anguar ……………………….69 to 88
Misery Personified on Anguar
Anguar Moon
Out of the Line
Anguar Cemetery
Claiming the Night
Long After the Battle
Shattered Shore
Anguar Goodbye
Lone Brave's Voyage
Walter Winemiller……………………………97 to 107
Ballad of Walter
On Iwo Jima
To Walter
South of the Sunset
Biggest Kill
Lone Brave's Dedication
Lone Brave's Fantasy
Lone Brave's Return
Trail Buddy Pardner
Regretful Trails
Requiem……………………………………..109 to 113
Veteran's Moon Sonnet
Too Many Memories
Dirge for the Dead
Taps
Glossary……………………………………..115 to 117

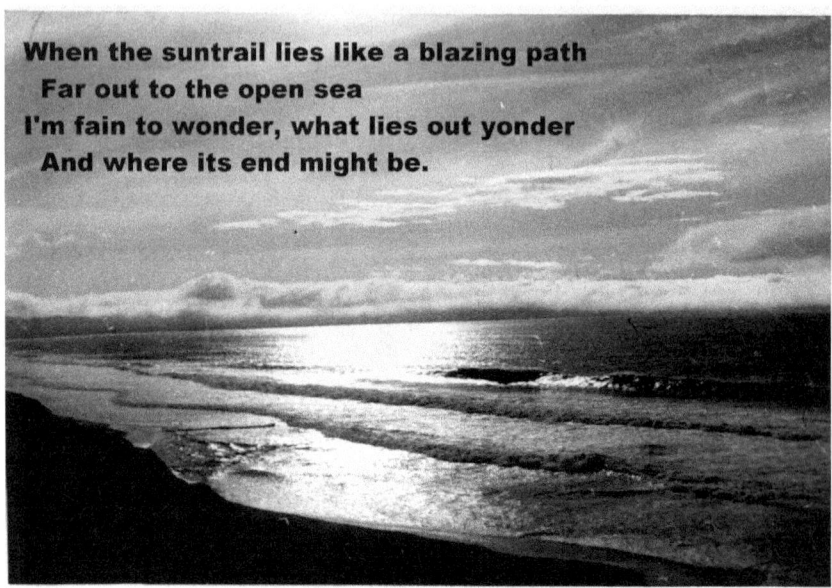

Suntrails on Pacific ocean

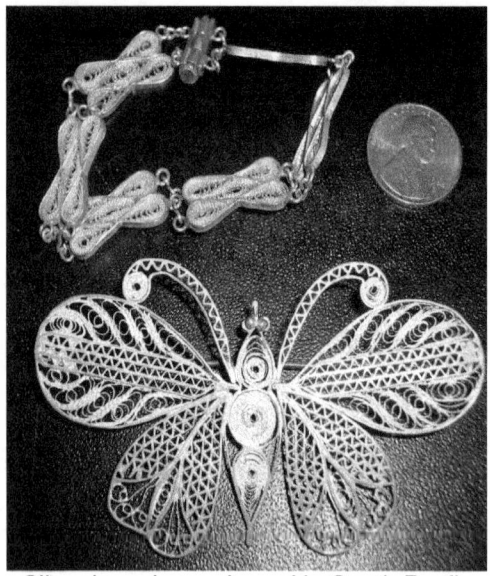

Silver jewerly purchased in South Pacfic
Photo Courtesy John Shaffer

When the suntrail lies like a blazing path
  Far out to the open sea
I'm fain to wonder, what lies out yonder
  And where its end might be.

AUTHOR'S PRAYER

Give me the words, dear Father,
Words that I can explain
All that I feel inside me
Of the weariness and pain.
Give me the words, dear Father.
Give me the skill once more
To tell the unawakened
Of the tragedy of war.

Give me the words, dear Father,
Words for the bitter years
Woven in starkest pattern
On a woof of unshed tears.
Give me the words, dear Father,
Only that they may know
What is the price of freedom
And why it is always so.

Give me the words, dear Father,
Grimly concise and clear,
Showing the deadly meaning
Of the wars of yesteryear.
Give me the words, dear Father,
Telling them one and all:
Heed to the solemn warning
Of the writing on the wall.

Give me the words, dear Father,
Telling the only way
Men can avoid the stigma
Of repeating yesterday.
Give me the words, dear Father,
Singing the only song--
Giving the only message
That can save the worldly throng.

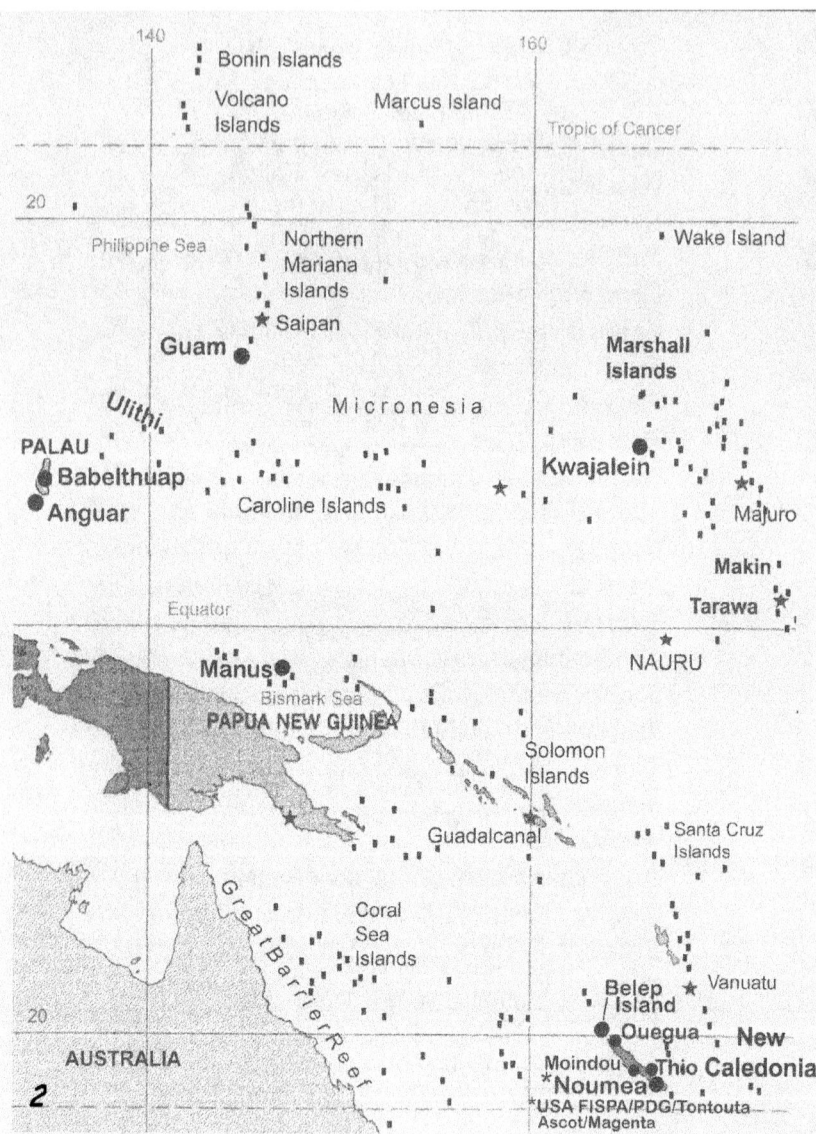

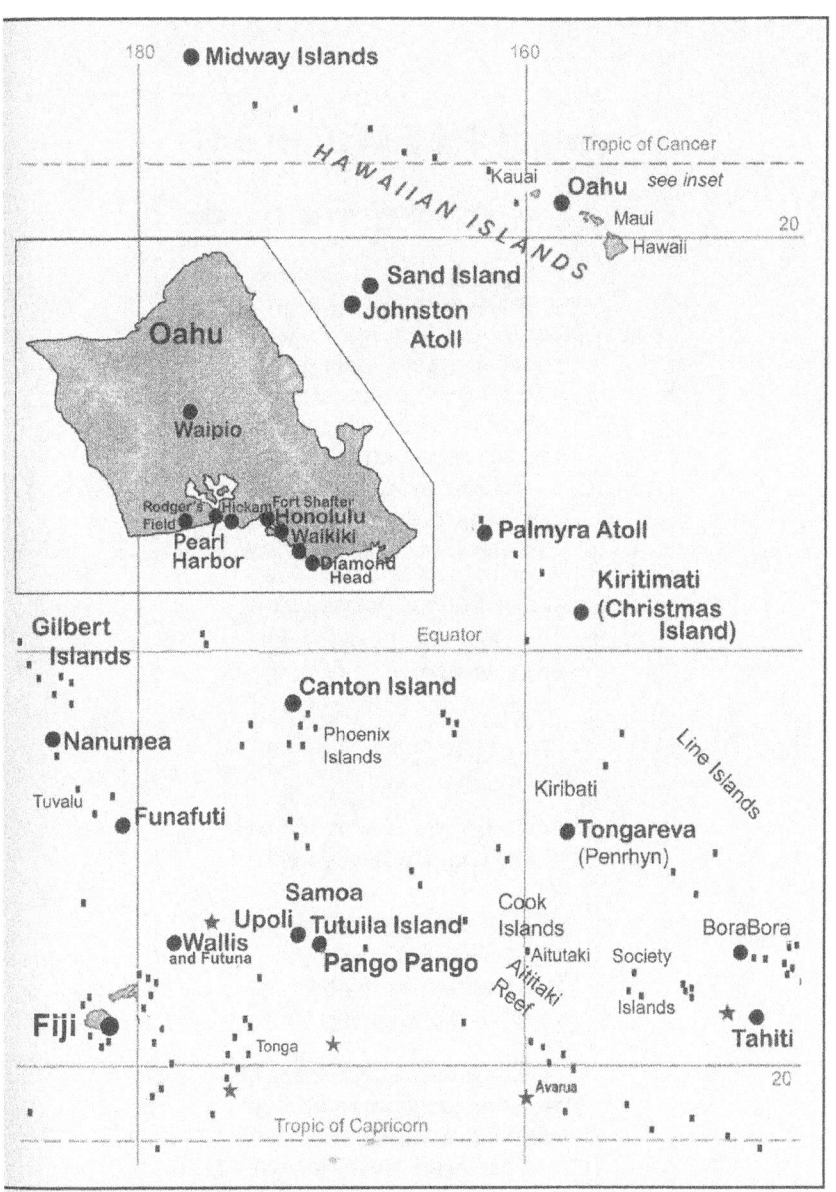

● indicates places where Earl spent time during the war. Other names are shown for general reference or because Earl referred to them in the "Doughboy Odyssey."

PREFACE

TELL'EM BEFORE THE DAWN

Tell 'em, they often told me.
Tell 'em we know you can.
Tell 'em about the Army
And the GI fighting man,

Not with the journal jargon
That the routine writers know--
But lyrical expression
Like the bards of long ago.

The journals tell of heroes
And the banners waving high,
But you must tell of pathos
And the way we live and die--

The loneliness and sorrow
That often strike us dumb
With thoughts about tomorrow
Whose dawn may never come.

TO UNDERSTAND

Tell 'em they often told me,
Tell 'em we know you can--
The way of the GI
And the lowly fighting man.

But how can I tell a story
That defies descriptive phrase?
And how can I tell a story
That's been lived ten million ways?

You've got to be a soldier
Before you understand;
You've got to be a soldier
Out in a foreign land.

You've got to sample misery
Alone and under stress;
Unsympathetic misery
For which there's no redress.

You've got to live the lonely
And unproductive years;
The years so blank and lonely,
And know a soldier's fears.

You've got to eat the rations
That never taste quite right;
And when there are no rations,
Just hitch your belt up tight.

You've got to starve and languish
Without the chance to quit;
You've got to starve and languish
And like it not a bit.

You've got to follow orders,
Though you know they're wrong.
You've got to follow orders
When punishment is strong.

You've got to do the bidding
Of someone you outclass;
You've got to do his bidding
And let the insult pass.

You've got to master patience
For wasted fruitless days;
You've got to master patience
In countless petty ways.

You've got to rudely banish
All trace of touchy pride;
You've got to roughly banish
And cast all hopes aside.

You've got to be a soldier
And bow to harsh command;
And if you're not a soldier
You'll never understand.

LONE BRAVE'S BONDAGE

Lone Brave went out to the Army
When the war clouds hovered near.
He left his native valley
In the springtime of the year.

The first of the buds were swelling
On the birch and maple trees.
Birds sang and the air was humming
With the buzz of honeybees.

He left the land of his childhood
For the distant paths of war
On the lonely jungle islands
Far beyond the western shore.

His heart remained in the mountains
And amongst the nearby hills.
His spirit was borne on pinions
Of the plaintive whip-poor-wills.

Out over the long tomorrow
He watches the years roll by--
In bondage to wrath and sorrow
Where death and destruction lie.

FOR CONSTANCY

Thousands of waves in every mile
And thousands of miles lie clear
Between this island of coral piles
And the land we love so dear.

Untold ripples on every wave
And waves that are never still
Between the shore where the South Sea lays
And where homeland breakers spill.

Thousands of thoughts that wing as one
Out over the troubled sea
To a native land from native sons
And voicing a single plea.

SOUTH OF THE SUNSET

Poetry of people, places, machines, work, and military maneuvers in the Pacific Theater of World War II

SULLEN PACIFIC

Out on the sullen Pacific
Covering half the world,
As pawns in a game gigantic,
Our dawning lives were hurled
Over the barrier water
Into a maelstrom of years--
Mingled with madness and slaughter;
Tangled with laughter and tears.

RADAR RACONTEURS

There's Tex and Sherman and Bobby
And Lyle and Eddie and me
Who travel with Mr. Sturdy
To work in the Southern Sea.

Radar Crew

Our job is installing radar
And getting it "on the air."
We build what they plan on paper
In a planning room somewhere.

Sturdy's the boss and promoter
And radio engineer.
Tex Davis installs the diesels
For power to "fire the gear."

The rest of us guys are GI's
Who serve as the working crew:
Uncrating, installing, wiring,
Whatever there is to do.

We work from dawn to sunset
And after when we have light.
When Tex has given us power,
We work in the dead of night.

The deadline is never distant;
We always must race with time
Way out at some lonely outpost
Not far from the battle line.

RADIO # 6

There's a rainbow on the ocean
And the day is cloudy fair
As the morning's work progresses
On an island anywhere.

Break out lots of stock materials
And unlock the kits of tools.
Get the air compressor working
And unreel the cable spools.

Dig the ditches and the guy holes;
String the feeder lines with care.
We're the radio construction
On an island anywhere.

A "guy-wire" work crew

TO MY CLIMBING BELT AND SPURS

When I'm high up on a palm tree
That's a-swayin' like a reed
When the earth seems far below me
And it's confidence I need,
Then my life is at your mercy
And it's you with whom I plead.

Spurs, keep diggin' deep and solid.
Keep me anchored firm and true.
Belt, my faith in you is stolid
For my weight is full on you,
And those rocks below look squalid
With no safety net in view.

Earl On Spurs

As a team you are the bulwark,
And as such I tritely say--
Constancy must be your trademark
At each whipsaw lurching sway,
For your grip upon this tree bark
Is my lease on life today.

HIGH LINER

Buckle that belt on and stuff her with tools
And strap on those climbers quick!
A couple of miles of new keyed lines
Is the job we have to lick.
And after that come some feeder lines
And new antennas to hang.
We're runnin' a race with deadline time
And only with half a gang.

You're weighed down with hammer and eight inch pliers,
A pole wrench and crescent, too.
Get up there and start to rig in' those wires;
There's plenty of work to do.
The hand line's unsnaggin'; dig in those spurs
And creep up to fix that gain.
Unbuckle that belt and slip 'er around.
(The moral of that is plain.)

Lay back in the harness and cinch her tight,
And sure as can be you're there.
You could be a climber--you're plenty bright--
Instead of just passing fair.
Watch out for those lines; they're blazin' hot.
Always prepare for the worst.
You'll soon be a lineman as like as not,
If work doesn't kill you first.

Lineman ready to climb

KAENA HIGH LINE

High up the hill, above the rocks
The cable line is slung,
Above the precipice that mocks
At the stoutest heart and lung.

Where truck or tractor cannot climb
Yet heavy loads must go--
A rocky crag with view sublime
Where constant breezes blow.

Yet grimly must the work progress
Though vehicles may shirk.
Regardless of the hard access
The high line does the work.

SWEATSHOP OF WAR

Sweaty and grimy with clothes soppy wet,
Sleazy and crummy as humans can get,
Laying out guy lines and ground rods and poles
On coral sand hot as a bed of live coals.

Measuring aerials, tightening lugs,
Wiping salt brine from our bewhiskered mugs,
Antenna systems seem destined to lie
In places where even a lizard would die.

Find a location on some meadow green
Where coral and palm trees have never been seen,
And leave but one thing we can grumble about.
I'll give you long odds that we'll ferret it out.

WAR WANDERERS

From the land of cane and pineapple
Of rainbow and of lei
To the lands that lie beneath the
Southern Cross,
We have flown and sailed the byways
Through the clouds and through the spray
In the kingdoms of the eagle
And the foam flecked albatross.

We have loitered on the beaches
And have scaled the barren hills.
We have visited the islands
One by one.
We have watched the tropic sunset
With the awe that it instills
And have squatted by the campfire
When the day's work all is done.

Now we've followed those same byways
Through the blue of sky and sea.
Back once more to where the North Star
Is the guide:
With the vastness yet before us
And the chance to go our plea---
To those many other places
Out beyond horizons wide.

There is nothing to deter us.
There is no place too remote--
We have been in isolated spots before.
We will ship in almost anything
That's fit to fly or float.
We but ask to pack our war bags
And to hit the trail once more.

ISLE OF POTTE

The clouds are like curly white lamb's wool
Scattered askance on the blue.
The palm fronds are green fans that rustle
And sway as the breeze trickles through.

The calm wavelets ripple and shimmer
Out on the coral lagoon,
While over toward the eastward
Hovers the first quarter moon.

Everything sunny and quiet,
Seemingly calm and serene,
Yet yesterday somebody sighted
An enemy submarine.

PARADISIAC

Out on Potte Island so happy and free
Tending the radar as pleased as can be,
Bouncing the truck up the lone thoroughfare
Free from all worry, homesickness, and care.

We fight for the chance to go on KP.
We wash pots and pans with greatest of glee.
We dig garbage pits while singing with joy
And service latrines with naught to annoy.

We never dispute; we always agree
The girls are all beautiful creatures to see.
We eat broiled steak and pie a la mode,
Not gallons of beans till we nearly explode.

We swim in the surf and lounge on the beach.
Yeah! Sit there and hear the gooney birds screech.
Six months of this and if you're huntin' me,
Look in the top of a coconut tree.

Earl on left and friends taking a break
from work for a little swim

TO BELEP

Island of Potte, it's *au revoir.*
You're fading in the haze,
A wraith like shadow sinking far
Beyond the keenest gaze.

You're fading fast into the past
As other such have done;
But so it is the die is cast,
A new trip is begun.

We make our way from isle to isle
But only passing through.
We've been with you a little while
And now farewell to you.

MAITAKI LAND BOY

Johnny boy, why do you want to go
Out from your island home--
It's Maitaki, too well I know--
To pack your bag and roam?

You had your friends and your way of life
Before our Army came.
Native boy, why should you want to stray
Out where the winds are tame?

The hurry and worry of the world
Isn't the thing for you.
They have their troubles as well as joys.
They are unhappy too.

They want to come to your little isles,
Out where the winds are free.
They call your island a paradise.
Johnny boy, don't you see?

LONG RANGE BOMBER CREW

The gaunt bombers squat in the gouged out revetments,
Grotesque in the shadows that filter the trees.
Hulks lacking in purpose if judged by appearance,
Yet vest with something that puts you at ease.

They're built like a boxcar, these big Liberators.
They're ugly and graceless from wingtip to core.
But out in the wide blue they're tough gladiators,
The kind of equipment that helps win a war.

On up to the cockpit the young pilot clambers
And nurses the throttle with sensitive touch
To quicken to thunder, the vast latent power,
That funnels the air in its swift whirling clutch.

The plane lumbers awkwardly out of its haven,
Out to the runway grotesquely and slow.
A thing brought alive by the men who are in her,
Pulsing with power and straining to go.

The motors are revved up to clear them for takeoff.
The ailerons waggled to see that they're free.
The crewmen don't relish the taking of chances,
Especially those that a check can foresee.

Mechanics have checked her, repaired her, and fueled her.
And now as she strains to the takeoff once more,
Her bomb racks are crammed with potential destruction
And fuel in her gas tanks to take her to war.

Her ponderous bulk seems so drudge like and weary
As wildly her props lash the air into fog;
'Til slowly she rises aloft with her burden
As steady and true as a faithful old dog.

And now let the tailgunner finish the story;
He told it one evening when going back out.
He's not one for metals or ballyhooed glory
But pretty well knows what the fighting's about.

The missions are long so we don't have an escort.
We fly from the Marshalls as far out as Truk.
Except for the fifties we have in our turrets,
There's nothing that we can rely on but luck.

The hours are so morbid and lacking and empty;
We're tired when we reach where the Zeros attack.
We fight for what seems as the space of a lifetime,
And wonder the while if we'll ever get back.

They hover about us and tip off the gunners;
They give them the height and the course and the speed.
Like vultures they circle and yet always wary,
And always the one who flies in the lead.

Then just when the ack-ack has pounded us groggy,
It stops and the Zeros swoop in for the kill.
They dive in succession down through our formation
Then zoom back again with tenacious skill.

We've got to stay up 'til the bomb run is over,
And then we drop down where a Zero can't dive.
They've got to have thousands of feet to recover
And that's about all that helps keep us alive.

But then they drop firebombs that burst in a shower
Of phosphorous over our low flying planes.
It burns like a torch when it contacts with metal
And leaves us to wonder what's taking the strain.

For thirty-five minutes the Zeros attack us.
So often I've timed them; it's always the same.
And then we limp home, that is if we're able,
    As pawns in the midst of a terrible game.

Blood plasma is useless to have when your buddy
    Is hit by a "20" that tears out his heart.
And what good are chutes when flying at zero
    And fire riddled structure at last falls apart?

One ship that we lost made a good water landing.
    I saw her go down from my place in the tail.
They launched their life rafts, but Zeros came swarming
    To strafe them though chances already were frail.

Another was hit as we covered the target.
    She burst into flame as we finished the run.
Her bombs fell away; her fuselage crumpled, and
Plunged down in the sea; but her mission was done.

The two that were lost were from our bomber squadron;
    And out of the eight men who bunked in our shack,
Six paid with their lives in that one single action.
    For only just two of us ever came back.

NANUMEA BOUND

With a parachute for a pillow
On a seat in a DC-3,
We're flying to Nanumea
Where the next job is to be.

We're crossing a stretch of water,
Where the Japanese patrol,
En route to the secret airbase
On Nanumea Atoll.

We swing in over the island
And hope that we're recognized.
Ships down below us are dodging
Not wanting to be surprised.

We waggle our wings in friendship
While feeling a trifle glum.
There's many a gun below us
Could blast us to kingdom come.

But word is flashed from the tower,
"All clear for a landing, friend."
We swing out wide for a landing
And come to our journey's end.

Shore of Nanumea

CORAL SEA SORTIE

White breakers slashing wildly
On shores abrupt and lone,
Starlight flickering mildly
On massive shapes of stone,
Sails full bellied by trade wind
Leaving Nanumea quay
Bound for a tiny island
Out in the Coral Sea.

NEGATIVE PARADISE

We wake to the roar of the dawn patrol
On our wee beloved isle--
To the crash of rolling combers
On the reefs far out to sea
And thrill to the deathless glamour
Of our barren coral pile
With all its recollections
That have been and are to be.

We wash in the barracks washing room
Where the faucets never run--
Then lounge on the comfy fixtures
Where the paper's always nil
And thrill to the priceless privilege
Of another day begun
As we dash toward the chow hall
Too late to eat our fill.

And thus by our lack of breakfast
And uncleanliness inspired,
We dash to the job encumbered
With a well contented smile
And add to the brisk confusion
That's so patently required
To bolster the lagging upkeep
Of our precious little isle.

Of course there's a bit of scenery
But it lacks the alpine touch.
And speaking of recreation,
There are movie shows and books.
And judging from what we're hearing,
We haven't been missing much
By stagnating on an island
So superior to what it looks.

So give us the roar of the dawn patrol
And the coral's blinding glare
And the flash of snow white combers
That rise above the reefs.

And give us your endless lectures
Of the privileges found here,
But we'll counter with the specter
Of its chronic lacks and griefs.

NEVER EASE

Rain, in a wild crescendo,
Through the black darkness
Upon the tent flap;
We douse the light
Then fall asleep.
Then suddenly
Awake,
The hair crawls
On my neck.
Is something,
Someone
Slowly, slowly,
Cautiously
Lifting the tent flap,
Hesitating,
Groping in the dark?
Taunt black darkness and rain
Beating in wild crescendo
Against the tent;
Lights out, we sleep restlessly.
Suddenly awake! Is someone slowly, slowly, cautiously
Lifting the tent flap, hesitating, groping in the dark?
Hair bristles on my neck.
On Guadalcanal, men were found throats cut--bled to
Death; necks severed at night.
A hand--heard it groping, feeling
Through darkness.
Its mate holding a knife or gun.
Grab the flap, snatch it up, don't wait.
Raise it now. Anything is better
Than waiting.
The night is still as death
Except the faint low sound.
Up with the flaps, eyes staring; nothing there
But a timely wind Stealing into the jungle.

BATTLE CRAZE

The hot green jungle teems with men.
The battle line is closely drawn
With just a skirmish now and then
But lasting on and on and on.

Tension is high, when suddenly
A lad with a long knife in his hand
Leaps from cover and recklessly
Crosses the narrow no man's land.

A foe springs up, a swinging thrust,
A broken stride, then raging on
To certain death as though he must--
Into the gloom, forever gone.

BATTLE GRAVES

Not even a cross on an island--
Not even a marking stone--
His body was never buried
And nothing definite known.
Ten yards from the foaming water
To the jungle growth of green,
Ten yards that he started crossing
And he died somewhere between.
Where is the young foot soldier?
Where does his body lie?
Somewhere between the ocean
And the jungle and the sky:
Wholly obliterated,
Vanished into the air,
Gone from among his comrades
And his grave is anywhere.
Graves on the lonely islands
Under a reeking sky,
Names that are fondly whispered
But the dead cannot reply.
Crosses of wood and white lead,
Each bearing a metal tag,
Lying in close formation
Neath their own beloved flag.

Where are the ones termed missing?
Who is the one unknown
Lying amidst the others
With no nametag of his own?
Where are the total records
And when shall the tally be--
Not till the final judgment
Somewhere in eternity.

NIUI CHROME

No modern array of colossal machines
Loads ore at Niui Bay.
From the tiny sluice mill that finally gleans
The ore from the lava clay,
Men shovel the ore into narrow gauge cars
And shovel it out again.
Then shovel it into the flat wooden barge
Which plies with the ship; and then
They shovel it into a bucket that's slung
By a winch overside.
And only the strong and sturdy young
Can handle the work in stride.
Javanese, Melanese, Polynesian, Malayan
Each race supplying a few,
A cross section group of the whole Southern Sea
All working on one small crew;
All loading the bucket that's dumped in the hold
And soon to be borne away.
The ore that in war is more precious than gold
Hand loaded at Niui Bay.

NOUVELLE CALEDONIA, ADIEU

We've gained new friends and experiences
While we sojourned on your shore.
We've learned the angles of travel
And we've learned the ways of war.

We've learned that the South Sea glamour
Is a lot of ballyhoo,
But we've learned that people live here
Much the same as others do.

We've seen that they have their cities
And their big department stores.
They have their farms and ranches
And their homes with hardwood floors.

But over the hill are hovels
Made of thatching gray or brown;
They have their tenement troubles
Just as we have shantytown.

We're leaving you, Treasure Island,
So strategic in the war.
We go with the sober knowledge
That we'll never see you more.

OLD JOE

Sixteen years as a lineman
And never finished a job,
Proud of his independence
As a boomer on the line.
Never the one for showoff
But the best hand in the mob;
Never appear to hurry
But commencin' mighty fine.

Strappin' a set of spurs on
And driftin' up a pole;
Bucklin' off and restin'
And smokin' a cigarette.
Cool, collected, and easy
While the other men cajole
But never another climber
Is up a pole as yet.

Always the first with tools on,
Always the first one done--
Never a reckless movement,
Always a careful job,
Always a line of chatter
Designed to start some fun,
Especially when it's raining
And the blues are playin' hob.

OUR SACRIFICE

We've given not only blood and sweat
And unshed aching tears,
But out of our youthful treasure
We have given precious years.
The years that we lose are Springtime
And the sowing time of life;
And we cannot reap good harvest
Mid gigantic weeds of strife.
Our strength is pitted against the threat
Of slavery or death;
And bodies and minds are broken
As the one sure aftermath.
The years of our youth are passed away;
The morning of life is lost--
Gone with the other and cheaper things
Summed up in the total cost.

BATTLE SCAR

He is branded for life by a long jagged scar
On the forehead and bridge of his nose.
Will it bring him respect where his countrymen are
As a sign of the valor it shows--
Of the numerous times when he stood by his guns
When the bomber was riddled and torn,
Of the AA barrage, and the low bombing runs,
And the Zeros he learned not to scorn?
Till one day when they couldn't get back to the base
And they made a crash landing at sea,
And his one souvenir is that scar on his face
Where the smooth of his forehead should be.
He is branded for life by that scar on his face,
A scar that is easy discerned.
Will it bring to him honor or senseless disgrace
From the people for whom it was earned?

BIGOTRY'S BALE

There are those who say a soldier
Is depraved and fallen low
Who know little more about it
Than a moron ought to know.
And they take the lone example
Of the one who's drunk and mean
And declare it universal
For the nine they've never seen.
Do they realize how stupid
And unjust their judgments are?
Do they realize how lonely
Are the men who travel far
To the last far dens of danger
At the government's behest
And were mustered to the service
As the country's chosen best?
Do they realize the bitter
State of mind their actions build,
And the unremitting sorrow
Their injustice has instilled?
Do they realize the magnitude
Of debt they really owe
To those they scorn and trample
As beneath their worth to know?

PACIFIC GRIPE

We'd like to ask a question,
General Marshall, Sir.
We boys were shown a movie
Two Down and One to Go.
They forced us all to see it
And in it talks occur
That leave some things unanswered
Of which we'd like to know.
You spoke of British transports,
General Marshall, Sir,
And how long absent Tommies
Should rate consideration.

Well, how about us, General?
We've been four years or more
Away without a furlough.
How about an explanation?
We never fought the Germans,
General Marshall, Sir,
So why should we be ordered
To see a movie show
About the wide Pacific
As though we never were
Out here and fighting Japanese
Since several years ago?
We've never had a furlough,
General Marshall, Sir,
Not even way back yonder
Before we crossed the seas.
Somewhere there must be blunders.
Somewhere the orders err.
We'd like an explanation
From you, Sir, if you please.
Too many points for furlough
And not enough for discharge,
Years on the forward islands
While all such places mean:
Away from home and family
For almost half a decade;
Caught in the chains of circumstance
And lost somewhere between.

SOUTH SEAS GLAMOUR TOUR!!

Far beyond the barren waters
Somewhere west of Pango Land
In amongst the groups of islands
That of late are Yankee manned
Lies one lonesome island
That perhaps is least of all
But their special service office
Must really be on the ball.

We were somnolently occupied
One long and boresome day
When we heard the howl of GI wolves
Across the taxiway.
When we boys investigated, we were
Struck by dumb surprise
For we saw some native women
Who had tried to glamorize.

They were decked in wild regalia
That were hula duds, I guess,
But beneath each scanty costume
Was a Mother Hubbard dress.
In their hair were festive garlands
Made of woven native grass,
And they'd smile and wave their pudgy
Arms at everyone they passed.

They were evidently touring
In a planned GI parade,
But the whole effect was satire
And not glamour, I'm afraid.
Though we tried through sheer politeness
To return their toothy smiles,
Still I rather doubt that anyone
Was captured by their wiles.

For they didn't much resemble
What the boys are fighting for,
And the commonest reaction
Was to double up and roar.
Yes, morale was greatly aided
By that South Sea glamour tour
For it ranked among the highest
as a sure-fire psycho cure!

THE DESERT ISLES

In tho bleakest part of an ocean
That is bleak from shore to shore
Encompassing half creation

In the far-flung island war,
Are islands of desolation
That thousands of men recall
As Midway, Baker, and Canton
And Johnston the worst of all.
We served on those tiny islands
Of coral and rock and sand,
Existing where plant life withered
And dreamed of our native land.
No trees where the shade could linger;
No grass where a man could lie
And trace with an idle finger
On the lacework of the sky.

No brooklets of cold clear water
But pits where the rising tide
Seeped through from the nearby ocean,
We lived and we lost our pride.
Embittered by endless yearning,
We clashed with relentless life:
In starkest clarity learning
The futility of strife.

There wasn't a chance for glory--
Just live on the sinking sand
As part of the horror story
That the mad warmongers planned.
In the bleakest part of an ocean,
We served on the desert isles:
Midway, Canton and Johnston
And Baker, the coral piles.

SOUTH OF THE SUNSET

South of the sunset in years gone by,
The sea could be calm or waves roll high.
South of the sunset on coral shores
Was ebb and flowing of island wars.
My heart is bound outward like petrel wings.
Sometimes it is broken; sometimes it sings.

Army Jeep

THE JEEP

There's been a lot of argument
About the Army jeep.
They tried to foist our little pet
With such a silly name as Peep.

They've stubbornly refused to let
Our pride and joy alone.
But we'll stand up for it, you bet,
And let the facts be known.

Around the world the jeep is found
In many diverse lands.
It covers lots of rugged ground
From rocks to shifting sands.

It's used for armed reconnaissance,
Equipped with radio.
"Blitz Buggy" is its alias;
There's no place it won't go.

It rides as smooth on bumpy ground
As big trucks on a road,
And never have the GI's found
What makes an overload.

It's known on every battlefront
For versatility.
It does whatever chore you want
With like efficiency.

It mounts a gun; it swims a stream;
With wings the thing would fly.
And just to ride it brings a gleam
To any soldier's eye.

With jealously we guard its fame.
With wrath our pulses leap
When someone tries to change the name
Of our beloved jeep.

THE LOW ATOLLS

Palm trees bathing in the moonlight
Combed by a gentle breeze;
Crooning a song at midnight
Beside quiescent seas.
Wailing of Banshee sirens;
The rending blast of bombs;
Terror and reflex action
To man the vengeful guns.

THE LUCK OF THE *BANSHEE'S WAIL*

Sure it brings to mind when a whining roar
Re-echoes across the sky
Of a fanciful and a less or more
Description of how they fly.
Now it's not heroic nor brave at all,
Not even a true-life tale;
And for want of a better name we'll call
"The Luck of the *Banshee's Wail*."

Now the *Banshee's Wail* was a pursuit job
That was flown by Pat Magee,
And her specialty was for play in hob
With the foes of Liberty.
And she seemed immune to the vicious lead
Though it flew as thick as hail,
For she thrived on luck as her skipper said,
"The Luck of the *Banshee's Wail*."

Now the *Wail* went up in the air one day
When the sky was full of planes.
And though Pat would fight in his own set way,
Still, he had more luck than brains.
For with flashing eyes and a low hummed tune
As he stalked a bomber's tail,
He would chant the praise of his bold Aroon,
"The Luck of the *Banshee's Wail.*"

They were out on a long patrol one day
And the skies were tender blue,
Like a colleen's eyes, smiling Pat would say,
For his loyalty was true.
And it must have seemed that he faced the end
When the breeze lashed into gale;
But he brought her in with, the boys contend,
"The Luck of the *Banshee's Wail.*"

Now the "Banshee's Wail" is the call of death
When it roams the heather lone.
Should you contemplate the aftermath
Of a fighter's wailing moan?
As to superstitious Pat Magee--
So his efforts could not fail--
Comes an answer clear as a soft macaque,
"The Luck of the *Banshee's Wail.*"

Banshee Wail in this poem is the name of Pat Magee's plane; however, the origin of the name came from an Irish folktale which has a wailing woman whose wails at death sound like a wailing owl. Pat Magee recites his own ballad about his plane, "The Luck of the *Banshee Wail,*" because of its wailing engine sound and narrow escapes. Please see the GLOSSARY for more details on this traditional Irish folktale. nn

THE MOVIN' PICTURE SHOW
On the loneliest of islands
Where there's little else for doing
At the far flung chains of bases
That our forces are accruing
O'er the vast globe girdling reaches
Where the Yankee fighters go,
You will find their recreation
Is the movin' picture show.

In the darkness after sunset
When the shadows bide projecting,
Like iron filings to a magnet,
You will see them congregating.
Though the picture may be ancient
And they've seen it long ago,
You will find them gravitatin'
To the movin' picture show.

By the twos and threes and dozens
They come drifting through the shadows--
Rawest rookies from the mainland
And the veterans of battles--
To escape the meditation
That's as lethal as a blow,
For a while to be forgetful
At the movin' picture show.

THE TRAIL OF MEN WHO KNOW

Out of the realm of men
Who do not dare to die--
Out of the darkness when
Men seek to reason why--
The trail of the men who know
And the spirit that never dies.
The trail of the men who show
It's destiny in their eyes
Leads out to the vast unknown
In search of the Hand that leads
Those few who are proud to own
The Faith that their questing breeds.
The crucible of the years
Is shaping them in its mold:
Robbing insatiate biers
Of plunder and wealth untold,
Keeping the reeling earth
From chaos and hopelessness,
Building the vast rebirth
That promises happiness.

Earl Shaffer's sister Anna endured a great disappointment and hardship in her life while Earl served in the South Pacific. He drew on his own personal disappointments and experiences to pen the following special poem of encouragement to her. nn

TO ANNA

Look high to the distant horizon;
Look out to the vastness of space,
And can thou not sense the uprising
Of prayers to the great Throne of Grace?

The greatest of God are the lowly,
Purged clean in the crucible fire;
And though the rewards come but slowly,
They transcend whatever transpire.

God uses us all for His namesake;
He chooses the means to employ.
And none who have never known heartbreak,
Can know the full meaning of joy.

May God as in Job's humble story
Grant faith and the insight to see
And use it at least for His glory,
Reserving a portion for thee.

THINKING OF HOME

It's night and the campfire is blazing
At close of a hectic day
And eyes that are raptly gazing
Screen thoughts that are far away.

A circle of men in the firelight,
A bivouac hasty and lone,
And each with a personal insight
To some little world of his own.

And hardships of war are forgotten;
Expelled are the cares of the day
As pleasanter thoughts are begotten
By memories of home far away.

It takes but the campfire soft gleaming,
No matter how far you may roam,
To set you to thinking sad dreaming
And bring you a vision of home.

Campfire on Belep

DUNNO

Dunno whether they haven't written,
Dunno whether it ain't got through,
Only know that I ain't been gittin'
Letters same as the others do.

Dunno whether they's all insulted,
Dunno whether they's all forgot,
Only know that I'm plain disgruntled
Waitin' round for I don't know what.

Don't know whether the sun is shinin',
Don't know whether they're still okay,
Only know that I'm sure a-pinin'
Wanting to hear from thataway.

Only wantin' to hear from you
Same as the other fellows do.

The family of Earl Shaffer does not know of a specific girl friend that he lost while overseas. Many of his war buddies asked him to pen poetry for special situations for them to send home. Perhaps this is such a poem in answer to an all too familiar wartime "Dear John" letter. nn

THE HARVEST OF WAR

There's a shadow across the moon trail
While writing this letter to you.
Your letter arrived in the noon mail
And left me heartbroken and blue.

For I've fathomed the undercurrent
Of things that you never quite say,
And at last I know what those words meant
Though said in a round about way.

You know that I never could blame you
That we have been drifting apart;
Though you know just as well as I do
That you reign as the queen of my heart.

It's been years since we've seen each other;
There are thousands of miles between.
Every time I move it's been further,
And I realize now what you mean.

There's little that war could be bringing
But heartache and sorrow and pain,
But couldn't your answer come winging
Back over the distance again?

I'm only a soldier who loves you--
For whom you had promised to wait.
I couldn't refuse, should I want to,
The freedom that you designate.

Your letter arrived in the noon mail
And here is the answer in part:
There's a shadow across the moon trail
And that shadow lies on my heart.

THIO PASS

One road leads up across the mountain
To Thio on the lonely northern shore.
It winds along the bleak niaouli canyons,
A roadway that has now been geared for war.

We took that road one day en route to Thio,
An overloaded truck and seven men.
We waited at the MP gate for clearance
Then started up the narrow road again.

We passed the highland homes of wealthy people
And the gray niaouli huts far down below
Where natives live and till the valley soil,
Ancestrally, since days of long ago .

Rain-softened road became a driving hazard.
We slid and nearly hurtled overside.
The trip that we started on so blithely
Was turning out to be a hectic ride.

But finally we came to downward grading.
The climax of our journeying was past,
And proud as any regiment parading
Our truck rolled into Thio town at last.

Road to Thio

TIDE LIGHTS

Through the moonlighted waters the long rollers sweep
Visitors wafted from out of the deep;
And off of the rollers the bright moonbeams glance
Like gossamer spirits that shimmer and dance
And play on your fancies like some weird séance
As beachward they gambol and leap.

And watching the moonbeams cavort at their play
Brings thoughts of the people who go the same way:
Who flutter a while like a moth in the flame
Seeking for glory and foot lighted fame,
Seeking a place in the light for their name,
Then vanish at close of the day.

But deep underneath, the currents run free:
Powerful, changeless, despite you and me.
Others have gone and now comes our turn
To carry the torch that ever must burn
And seek for the glory for which we all yearn,
But most of us never will see.

Deep are the currents of sea and of life,
Constant and changeless through pleasure and strife.
Though small variations may constantly show--
Though tragedy threaten or wild tempest blow--
Still deep underneath, the calm waters flow
Though storms on the surface run rife.

Thus we, like the breakers that ceaselessly roll
Though constantly seeking a self chosen goal,
Are wafted along on the effortless tide
That cannot be bested though often defied
And relegates mortals to ever abide
As myriad parts of the whole.

TO A FOXHOLE

Dear little cave, I love you.
When the bomber moon rides high,
I'm always thinking of you
When I hear a plane go by.

The cradle moon is growing,
Waxing fuller night by night,
And too well are we knowing
Who is guided by its light.

Dear little foxhole haven,
You're the pinnacle of worth
When man becomes a craven
And must seek old Mother Earth.

Dear little cave, I love you
For the moon is full tonight.
With my two hands I dug you,
And your palm log roof is tight.

Sheer work and sweat have made you.
You're my honest pride and joy.
There's naught for which I'd trade you
When the fleeing host deploy.

Dear little foxhole haven,
Let me linger by thy side
When comes that honest craving
For a good safe place to hide.

The moon has started waning
And no bombs have come as yet;
But no one is complaining,
Just the opposite, you bet.

The veterans have told us
That the bomber moon is prime
When it hovers at the zenith
In its week of waning time.

For early hours of morning,
With the late moon high above,
When men least heed a warning
Is the time the bombers love.

Dear little cave, I love you.
Though the new moon now is nigh,
I still keep thinking of you
When I hear a plane go by.

Earl's Foxhole

FOXHOLE PRAYER

Dear God, forgive the way I was.
I spoke of Thee with scorn.
I know Thee now as each one does
Whose faith is battle born.

No atheist, if such there be,
Could ever dare deny
That man must turn in fear to Thee
When bullets whistle by.

Dear God, I know I have not earned
The right to make this plea:
To grant me now the thing I spurned,
A closer bond with Thee.

NUISANCE RAID

With my carbine across my belly
And my bush knife in my hand,
I'm huddled under my poncho
By my slit trench in the sand.

The rain drums hard on my shoulders
And the night is sultry warm
While the hum of Nippon motors
Dimly rides above the storm.

For hours a plane had dawdled
Out beyond the range of flack
Just to keep us by our foxholes
While the rain runs down our backs.

Hours pass by while bodies shiver
Though the danger may be slight;
And taut nerves are all a-quiver
With the madness of the night.

And the nimble thoughts go roving,
And the web of memory weaves
In a slow haphazard jumble
Until "Midnight Charlie" leaves.

TO JOHN MAGEE

You wrote a sonnet far up in the sky
While flying patrol in a fighter plane,
Singing of sunshine and cloud bannered sky,
Witnessing God in his far-flung domain,
Not knowing that soon was your time to die
Before you could ever use pen again.
Facing the hazards of death unafraid
Far in the blue of the special air,
Climbing the heights of a zephyr parade
Free from the despond of sad eyed despair,
Awed by the tranquil you gratefully prayed
Praising your God in the silences there.
John Magee, if all knowledge were time,
The whole world would sing such sonnets with you.

Pilot Officer John Magee
Photo Courtesy Wikipedia

TO MOTHER MULDOON

Sure Jimmy has the blarney
And the color of the skies
A-shinin' through the lashes
Of his laughin' Irish eyes.

The map of Ireland on his face
He couldn't help from havin'
For sure his mother had her home
In Erin's County Gavin.

Your Jimmy's heart's in Brooklyn
Where 'tis sure he'd rather be
For he's thinkin' of his mother
Though he's far across the sea.

It's a lot he would be givin'
To be goin' home tonight,
To see the streets of old New York
With all their gleaming light.

And find the peace of home sweet home
That seems so far away
And yet lives on in fondest dreams
Of going back someday.

CAPTAIN WERMUTH

Captain Arthur Wermuth became known as the "Ghost of Bataan" for his heroics in the Philippines before and after his capture by the Japanese. nn

"A potent one man army,"
His buddies proudly said.
And he alone had tallied
A hundred sixteen dead.
Alone he prowled the jungle,
Reconnaissance his aim
But ever on the lookout
For slant-eyed yellow game.
Though many Japs contested

Capt Wermuth
Photo Courtesy Wikipedia

But few lived through the fight,
For doomed was any foeman
Who framed his battle sight.
A Tommy gun his weapon
And steady nerves of steel,
And daring flaming courage
That made the Nippons reel.
He was but one of many
Who fought despite despair,
And stories of their exploits
Are broadcast everywhere.

And though he has been captured,
A prisoner of war,
Still many more will follow
Where he led on before.
And if we each accomplish
Just part of what he's done,
The foe cannot withstand us
And peace will soon be won.

TO TEX DAVIS

The words come slow and painful, Tex,
That always came so free.
Just seems as though I can't express
The deep inside of me.

And yet, I'm sure there is no need
To voice what we both know--
True friendship yields its honest mode
Though choice of words be slow.

A few short months we "gang the braves"
Beyond the Southern Sea;
And yet we found a thousand ways
Our thoughts and hopes agree.

And though we never meet again,
Which is I hope untrue,
I'll always claim you as my friend
And be the same to you.

Then thank you, Tex, for those few words
Of praise and inspiration.
And may God grant to you and yours
His fullest benediction.

TRACER SONG

What do the flaming tracers say
That flash out through the night,
Ribbons of fire that arch away
In streaming crimson light?
What do they say to friend or foe,
Ominously in voices low,

Greedily clear as on they go?
"We are the Guides to show the way;
We are the Messengers of night.
We would block out the Milky Way
And guide grim Death aright."

UNDER ONE MOON

The moon is riding high on an ocean of cloud tonight
Lending a measure of charm to our barren little island.
There are many other places that lie in its lunar brilliance
Exposed perhaps as starkly and no less amply flattered
Is the vast perimeter of bases stretching from the Marshalls
On down to New Guinea and Australia and India.
The men are joking forebodingly of "Washing Machine Charley"
And longing for the same moon over the Golden Gate.
From those same lonely bases, the bombers are lifting
To seek out the yellow foemen who also fear the moon.
Muddy, bedraggled infantrymen are huddled in their foxholes
In the jungles of New Guinea, New Britain, and Bougainvillea
Groping with ears and eyes for the elusive enemy.
In once romantic Burma, resounds the din of a death struggle.
And high in the mountains of Italy are half-frozen doughfeet
Advancing against equally cold and homesick Germans.
The hardy Russians are floundering through frigid blizzards
Exterminating as many Nazi soldiers as possible.
Vast armadas of planes are blasting each other into wreckage
Over the bomb shattered cities of England and Europe.
And out on the high seas of all the far flung oceans,
Submarines stalk the convoys in deadly determination.
And back in the homelands, en route home from the war plants
of America, England, Russia and all the other countries--
Doing the farm chores and guarding forests and war factories,
And all the other complexities of modern warfare:
Watching, waiting and praying, working, walking, and loving.
The young, the old and the lonely--wondering, hating, hoping—
Millions and millions and millions, all under one moon,
And over it all, one moon.

ATOLL EVENSONG

In the vesper time of evening
When the sea flows molten gray,
Comes a whisper from the gloaming
To explore without delay
All the thoughts that have full meaning
At no other time of day.

In a mind set free of bondage
By the canopy of gloam,
Are the seeds ripened for tillage
In a bed of fertile loam,
Thriving thriftily on pillage
From a vast unwritten tome.

Will we ever find fulfillment
Of the promise in that song?
Will we see a vast curtailment
Of the potency of wrong?
Will our sorrows find interment
In the past where they belong?

UNDER THE SHELL

He's writing a letter across the way.
There's only a table between.
He's tough as a whip, some folks would say,
A young hardboiled Marine.

But now as he forms the close penned page
There's heartbreak in his eyes,
And his twitching lips and tender age
Betray what underlies.

He's only a kid who's far away
From where he'd like to be,
A homesick boy whose hopes are gray
Beyond a dismal sea.

UTTER DESECRATION

They passed in a wave of smoke and flame
Fighting and bleeding, dying and dead.
Uniformed robots, pawns in a game,
Gaining a beachhead, the papers said.

They reach a jungle of loathsome mud
Doggedly groping through darkling fears
For courage bravely to shed their blood,
Spending the hours that seem like years.

They pass in a wave of smoke and flame
Leaving the dead and the dying behind.
Trained to duty by number, not name;
Chained to that duty by crass mankind.

Disciplined harshly to fight and die--
Forced into conflict by circumstance,
Sidestepping corpses and passing by,
Hardening hate in their frenzied glance.

They pass in a wave of smoke and flame
Over the beaches of blood covered sand,
Pawns being spent in a vicious game,
Far from the fields of their native land.

VANDAL MOON

I look at the moon and its silvery light
Has the brilliance it had before.
I gaze at the stars and they shine as bright
As they did in the days of yore.

But the same full moon is a bomber's moon
When the eggs of death are laid;
And the same starlight is a welcome boon
To the flash of a naked blade.

There are forces loose that would fain destroy
The spirit that's wild and free;
But it flares anew with exultant joy
In defiance of tyranny.

WARUM?

There's a weather beaten cemetery
Underneath the palms,
Impassively neglected by the great
Turmoil of war,
That seems hidden in the vestries
Of a host of whispered psalms
From lips of those who've languished
On this uninviting shore.
There are crosses there by dozens
That are moldered and decayed

Warum Stone

By humid tropic weather.
And the monument of stone,
Where once burnished gray memorials,
Bears just one block lettered word.
A word that seems engendered by a
Faith rejecting groan.
On the plain, ungarnished surface of that
Spacious granite face,
The vast soul burdened anguish of a
Sorrow-stricken dumb

For another who had perished in this
Lone-forsaken place:
Just the one word in remembrance,
The single word "Warum?"

**Warum is a German word that means WHY?
Many of the islands were German territories in the late 19th and early 20th centuries before being occupied by the Japanese. nn**

BATTLESHIPS

Where wild waters mirror the mood of the sky
Through sunlighted azure or storm-cloudy gray,
Where tall wind clouds saunter so jauntily by
Half casting their shadows in frolicsome way,
The gallant ships venture to hazard and die—
To vanquish or vanish in course of the fray.
Where decks are of armor, not hardwood and wax,
And cargo is cannon and powder and shell.
Where strength dare not waver nor vigil be lax,
And fear is a weakness to ruthlessly quell.
Where virtue means valor in facing attacks
Whose outcome no mortal can surely foretell.
Sing low in the rigging, O Wind of the Sea,
The decks and the gunpits are reeking with red.
The torn ships are sinking in hapless melee.
The turrets are shattered; the gunners are dead.
New battles are raging, new orgies to be .
Old wakes are behind us; new wakes lie ahead.

WHO JUDGED THE TIDE?

At the beachhead on Tarawa,
In that great ill timed fiasco,
When the landing boats were stranded
And the troops must charge by wading
Up against the Jap pillboxes:
Plunging headlong into pockets,
Losing time and their equipment.
Then who was it set the schedule?

Judged the time and gave the orders
To debark? Who judged the tide?
Just an almanac is needed
To learn when the tide is changing.
Lives are costly, not for wasting
By someone who isn't careful.
Higgins boats are landing barges--
They're not ducks or alligators.
They must have their draft on water.
They are only man's machinery.
They could never do the judging
Of the time. Who judged the tide?

DIRGE OF THE LANDING BARGE

The guns were spittin' chunks of lead
Over my head
Toward the shore--
That burst high up into the air--
To rip and tear
The island's core.

Machine guns chatterin' and sprayin'--
Busy layin'
A tight barrage;
Spillin' the empty cartridge shells
Like peanut hulls
In wild hodge-podge.

Close to the shore came mortar fire
And tangled wire
In barriers;
Till on the beach at last I strode
To spew my load
Of warriors.

They fanned across the rocky beach
Until they reached
The battle line.
And I turned back toward the ship
To make the trip a second time.

And now along the reef I lie
Beneath a sky
Of smoke and flame,
Torn to the heart and left to die--
Expendably,
Without a name.

ADVANCE BASE

Angry surf is never quiet
Out toward the northern sea
Where beyond the far horizon
Lurks the wily Japanese.
On another pinpoint island
Up a hundred miles or so
He has builded him an airbase
As our men have cause to know.
Bombs have burst on Nanumea
And they soon will burst again.
But the men have been preparing;
And they'll be more ready then
When from out beyond the breakers
With their constant clash and roar,
Little yellow men come skulking
In the deadly game of war.

A VOICE FROM FLANDERS

Mid heat and dust and battle din
With all its frenzied sound,
When weariness is deep within
And rest cannot be found;

When duty doesn't leave you choice,
Yet strength and hope are gone;
The whisper of an inner voice
Says, "Doughboy, carry on.

"We too must fight to our last breath
And then fight on some more.
We too were faced with blood and death
Back in that other war.

"We too found strength to fire the gun
When all our strength was gone.
And only cowards break and run.
So, Doughboy, carry on.

"It isn't feeling fear that's bad;
It's letting fear have sway.
For fear is something all have had,
The brave but choose to stay.

"The coward flees when things get rough,
And all his hopes are gone.
But you're a man who's man enough;
So, Doughboy, carry on."

CHANCE REUNION

Two men are in the tent tonight
With voices throttled down
In sotto accents making talk
About the old hometown.

They speak of marriages and deaths
And someone's baby girl,
Of church affairs and relatives
Of home and social whirl.

Two men who speak in sotto tones
About the folks they knew,
While far and clear the siren drones
And death awaits its cue.

DREAD SOUVENIR

In dead of the night I'm back again,
Back down in the island war,
Hunched down in a shallow fox hole
On a bleak shell splintered shore.
My carbine is cocked and ready
And I'm watching for a Jap,
Expecting a short fused hand grenade
To land right in my lap.
Howitzers, mortars and "fifties"

Are serenading the night.
Above are the green-eyed star shells
Providing their ghastly light.
My eyes are staring in vigil
And my ears are tuned to hear
That slightest of stealthy movement
When a Jap is creeping near.
There's thunder and creeping shadows,
Grim silence and deep despair;
And out to the Great Almighty
Goes a softly worded prayer.
Mosquitoes and death and lightning;
Gunfire and star shells and rain;
Motor hum high in the cloud banks--
Bomb bursts, then vigil again.
Quick staring at shifting shadows
Where the jungle creatures creep;
Crouched down in awkward discomfort
And fighting the demon sleep.
Deep dead of the night and back again
In the same old coral hole
Listening, watching, and waiting
While the big guns crash and roll.
Mind verging on loosened madness,
Nerves taut as a shrilling scream.
Then I wake up in the darkness
And find it was just a dream.

BENEVOLENT CASTIGATION

Ye of America, you cannot know
How it is facing the wrath of the foe.
Bombs have not torn you, gun or grenade.
You have no concept how warfare is played.
You are our loved ones, yet we must say
You do not know what war is today.
War is the bursting of bombs all around:
Noise so terrific you can't hear a sound;
Man-made destruction, desolate woe.
You in our homeland have no way to know.
Think of the viewpoint of doughboys who live
Out in a pup tent that leaks like a sieve:
Food of necessity often is poor;

Clothing worn out and the water impure;
Watching and waiting through infinite hours
For poisonous fogbanks and dynamite showers;
Constant alerts for a possible charge--
Watching a beach for an enemy barge;
Creeping through bushes like stalking for deer,
Knowing full well that the foemen are near;
Flying a plane through the deathladen skies,
Playing a game with death as a prize;
Manning a gun on a bomb ridden ship,
Watching the wing on your pursuit plane rip;
Facing sure death in a myriad ways;
Moments slow passing as long endless days.
Say not that you know how the agencies feel;
You have not fought with the cold bladed steel.
How could you fathom the life in a camp:
Everything muddy and dirty and damp;
Countless discomforts and sacrificed whims;
Heartbroken rookies with jellified limbs;
No chance for choosing a thing that you do;
No Chance for giving your own point of view?
Rise up America! Rouse from your sleep.
Long is the labor; the ascent is steep.
Precious the red blood that still must be shed.
Many the soldier that soon will be dead.
The longer you dally before you wake,
The more men must die and the longer must take.
No petty quarrels must stand in the way--
Politics long since has outlived its day--
Gunfire and bomb burst only can teach.
How can you know where the bombs never reach?
Fervent our hopes that you never will know,
Never will feel the mad wrath of the foe.
Wake to the fact that you don't know it now.
Make to yourself an unbreakable vow
That you will do what you possibly can
Keeping you faith with your own fighting men.

FRANKLIN DELANO ROOSEVELT

In the times of greatest conflict
When emergencies arise,
When our course must be heroic
Else we perish otherwise;
In the dominant position
There must be a man to choose
When a difficult decision
Means the choice of win or lose.

In the past such men have mustered
To our country's urgent call
And about those men have clustered
Strength and will to save us all.
Washington and Lincoln, mainly,
Each fulfilled his country's need;
And their worth is written plainly
In the history books to read.
And now once again the conflict
Called for leaders to the fore
With the grim and deadly prospect
Of a greater global war.
Franklin Roosevelt was chosen
And he did the best he could;
And events have simply proven
That the course he chose was good.

Then along the road to freedom
With the chart marked well ahead,
In the tower of his wisdom
He has joined our honored dead;
Not to see the final triumph
Over tyranny and greed,
Not to lead us in the pageant
That will crown the finished deed.

To see his plan evolving
To that final open door
When the nations come to solving
All the outlawry of war.
Man of destiny accomplished,
He has earned his high acclaim;
And his memory unblemished
Joins the stellar Hall of Fame.

GRAVE ON GUADALCANAL

My picture is standing against a cross
On a grave on Guadalcanal
In the tangled jungle of vine and moss
At the end of a bloody mile.
He carried my picture along with him
On the crest of the battle line.
He was just a private with purpose grim,
But the love of his heart was mine.
And I would that I could be lying there
In the place where my picture lies,
For life is a burdensome thing to bear
When the one who inspires it dies.

In the above poem, Earl is empathizing with one of the homeland survivors. nn

ISLAND WAR

The islands are scattered widely
On the bosom of the sea,
Far-flung and defended blindly
By the tensile Japanese.
Out there where the strong are leaven
And a man must show his worth,
We met with the "sons of heaven"
And we brought 'em down to Earth.
The shores are of rock and coral:
Washed by countless ocean waves,
Closely bounded by the jungle,
Interspersed with shallow graves.
Beaches torn into a shambles
By the bomb size naval shells
Where the leach-like sniper scrambles
And the hidden gun excels.
The reefs are a hostile network
That capsize a landing barge--
Too shallow to storm the bulwark,
Yet too deep for men to charge--
No cover and no protection
From the fiendish mortar fire.

Just stumble the right direction
Over rocks and tangled wire,
And even the ones who make it
To a foothold on the shore
Are only an open target
Oozing fear from every pore.
They plunge in a headlong scramble
Where the stern defenders hide,
And life is only a gamble
That the fates of war decide.
The heat is a ghastly choking
And their eyes are blind with sweat.
They crawl in an endless groping
And the battle young as yet.
Mosquitoes in swarms surround them
And they dare not move to slap
With always that fear around them
Of the hidden sneaky Jap.
They crouch in the lonely foxholes
When the first foothold is won,
Suspicious of every shadow--
Keeping watch with ready gun.
For days there is never sleeping
But the constant battle strain:
The crouching and stealthy creeping,
And the fever and the rain.
The Japs have the better training
And they know the country, too;
But still the defense is waning
And their numbers now are few.
Our power is overwhelming
As we press home the attack.
The tide of the fight is changing
And the Japs are falling back.
They hide in the caves and canyons
For the last ditch battle stand.
We know, and we're mighty thankful,
That the end is near at hand.
Out there where the strong are leaven
And man must show his worth,
We met with the "sons of heaven";
And we brought 'em down to Earth.

LAST STOP INTERLUDE

We lay in the most bedraggled
of a row of battered tents
And breathed of the night air's vagrance
through a host of shrapnel rents.

Our atrophied bunks were sinking
in a floor of oozing mud,
And the full moon shone upon us
in a bright betraying flood.

They'd christened the place Death Valley
and it's easy reckoned why--
For it's there the bombs come thumping
when the high moon rules the sky.

A batch of Torpedo pilots--
headed out toward the fray--
Were languishing there beside us
in a pause along the way.

Only kids of barely twenty
yet they each wore shavetail bars;
And I somehow started thinking
of their future battle scars.

They were painting bright word pictures
of the vivid stateside scenes
In a way that sounded strange indeed
for Officer Marines.

Till their homesick voices faded
to a silence all forlorn,
And the last declared he'd settle
for a bag of fresh popcorn.

LEAKY MORALE

Let's digress about the Army.
Let us turn aside awhile
To the problems military
Most pertaining to morale.
Let us probe with scanty mercy
To the bottom of the pile.

Just what makes an Army happy?
What will cause *Esprit de Corps*?
What will keep 'em dressin' snappy;
Make 'em reenlist for more?
What will keep 'em hep and scrappy--
Be it peace or be it war?

Is it pay or is it quarters?
Is it food that they expect?
Are such petty things the answer
Or are reasons more direct?
Is it taking proper orders
From a man they can respect?

Yes, that's what it is exactly--
That's the secret of it all.
If he handles 'em correctly
He can keep 'em on the ball.
If he treats them circumspectly
Their *esprit* will never pall.

An Officer should be chosen
On the basis of a creed
Whereby merit must be proven
To the men that he will lead,
With no hidebound caste distinction
From which despotism breeds.

It's the makeup of the Army
In an antiquated style
With its "Act of Congress" coterie
Who exploit the rank and file
That prolongs the oligarchy,
Chiefly causing low morale.

TARNISHED BRASS

There's lots of tarnished brass around
These Army camps of ours.
The trouble is it's mostly found
Amongst the ruling powers.
It's the kind that bears no polishing
Yet reeks with green corrosion,
And attempts at brash abolishing
Result in sure explosion.
There's a Major in the Signal Corps
Who rates a yardbird's pay,
Yet has a lot and thirsts for more
Authority each day.
Every soldier in the outfit
Is a heap more on the ball,
And the so-called Major's worth is such
He's worse than none at all.
He doesn't seem to realize
We're here to fight a war.
He acts as if he's super wise
And knows the total score,
Though no one seems to quite agree.
But then what can they do?
He wields the rod and wields it free
To subjugate the true.
He transfers all subordinates
Who dare to disagree.
Those who remain he subjugates
To bend the servile knee.
No one may speak a single word
That dares to criticize,
But praise no matter how absurd
Is merited as wise.
Such tarnished brass is hard to shine.
It's better to replace
At forward island battle line
Or stateside training base.
But why have any brass at all
But leaders tried and true
Who keep an outfit on the ball
And work the same as you?

MEN O' WAR

The men o' war are flying high
Against the cobalt blue;
Black silhouettes against the sky
En route to places new.

Why do they come from out the west
In such a multitude?
Perhaps they go to build their nest
And hatch and raise their brood.

But other men o' war have come
To Tongareva's isles;
The music of their motor's hum
Has crossed the ocean miles.

They too pass on but to the south--
Their drone to never cease--
To lay eggs in the cannon's mouth,
And hatch the dove of peace.

The men o' war are flying high
Like aeroplanes in flight.
On tireless wings they soar on by
On wings as black as night.

May they in all their freedom find
What men so seldom know;
And may we, too, gain peace of mind
And right to live and grow.

UGLY DUCKLINGS

The bronze of the ragged sunrise
Is a tangled cloudbank tower
Uplifting the languid stillness
Of the coral island scenes
When the clustered groups of bombers
In a thunderous surge of power
Roar across the western shoreline
Off toward the Philippines.

They are clumsy looking creatures;
Are the workhorse Liberators.
There is nothing sleek or lovely
In their awkward fuselage,
But they haul the dead weight tonnage
On the long range bomber sorties.
And they get across the target
And survive the ack barrage.

They'll be back perhaps by evening
When the shadows start to lengthen;
Coming swiftly through the sunset
Tired and eager to descend
To the refuge of the home base,
And the chance for relaxation
That a war bird needs so tensely
When it comes to mission's end.

The above poem refers to the B-24 Liberator bomber.

END OF THE DAWN PATROL

When the sun peeps from the ocean
At close of the dawn patrol,
The fighters come Indian filing
Through a perfect Immelmann roll;
Then turn from reversed direction
Diving down to complete the loop
And barrel roll in succession,
While maintaining the same tight group.
They join in an arc of streamers
From their own white vapor trails
In a last tight turning flourish
As the golden sunrise pales,
Streaking low across the island
To complete the serial show;
Then swing wide to settle slowly
To the airfield down below.

QUEEN OF THE SKIES

B-29 Bomber
Photo Courtesy Wikipedia

Lean, grayish shapes touched with silver highlights,
Wolfish and grim as they lie at rest
On the fields of Guam as we pass at midnight
Biding the time of their coming quest.

Sprawling and huge and deceptively slender
Coming to life at the break of dawn;
Fueled and well loaded with deadly provender,
They climb the sky and are swiftly gone.

Flying the way of the war bird's mission
Far to the North where the target lies--
Swiftly and surely to wield destruction,
Our B-29, the Queen of the Skies.

GRUMMAN WILDCAT

A pop, then a coughing rumble,
Then a deep full throated roar
That still has a trace of grumble
For a half a minute more.

Then it steadies into thunder
And it seems to beat its breast
Tearing silences asunder
With a wild exultant zest.

Lifting wings of jaunty gamecock,
But of much more somber hue,
Past the sea breeze bellied windsock
Up into the vaulted blue.

Zooming swiftly up a cloud bank
But to turn its nose and dive
With a scream as of its namesake,
Or a death's head come alive.

Raising dust along the airstrip
Causing trees to wave and shake
While it lets its stubby wings dip
Till it seems the prop must break.

Though it's not a classic beauty
As some other fighters claim,
It's a stickler to its duty;
And it lives up to its name.

SOMETIME THE DAWN

Sometime must come the dawning
Though long and lone the night.
The force of wrong, though vast and strong,
Must yield at last to right.

Though treachery may give an edge
To foemen in the fight,
It cannot match an honest pledge
Fulfilled by honest might.
The might that only comes to those
Who labor long and hard:
Who purge dissension, laugh at woes,
And keep their faith unmarred.

Who always keep their efforts aimed
At winning in the strife--
Avenging killed and raped and maimed,
Each lost or ruined life.

Who will not shrink although they know
That they themselves might die.
Whose only thought is beat the foe--
"We'll win" their battle cry.

Sometime must come the dawning;
And though we know not when,
A bright new day is on its way
When we'll have peace again.

WORLD WAR II WAR JOURNALISTS

Sgt. Howard Brodie

Sketching the jungle fighters
In graphic close up style,
Heedless of constant danger
Where stealthy snipers prowl.
Having his pad of sketches
Shot from his outstretched hand,
Such are the "journalistics"
The battlefronts demand.

Sgt. Mack Morris

Wholly unknown to the Hall of Fame
Except to the trade unknown,
Never vouchsafing the slightest claim
For bravery of his own,
An unassuming and quiet man
That few would recognize
As one of the long neglected clan
Who truthfully journalize.
He covered the island battlefront
Back "then" when comforts were few
As one of the few who bore the brunt
Of writing the news for you.
A correspondent in uniform
Who started when "Yank" began
And had more time in the foxholes
Than many a combat man.

To Ernie Pyle

Ernie Pyle
Photo courtesy of Wikipedia

There's a column seen no longer in the papers,
And the clippings in the letters come no more
For he's gone who forged in literary capers
An expression for the deep pathos of war.
Plodding grimly with the doughfoot in the foxholes,
Writing always in an easy humble style,
He has gone to join the ranks of other heroes.
And we bid farewell to little Ernie Pyle,
Yet his spirit still will always be beside us
In the boondocks where our fallen buddies lie.
And the understanding others have denied us
Has been written in a way that cannot die.
Ernie Pyle was not the one to speak of glory
In the gilt and glitter way that falsifies,
But he told straightforwardly the honest story
Of the way a common soldier lives and dies.

PACIFIC CONVOY

The blue of the ocean, the white of the foam,
The blaze of the sunset red----
The colors that proudly wave over our home;
The land where our freedom was bred.

Deep blue is the water through which we are sailing,
An endless expanse of turquoise;
As onward we go with the foe unavailing,
Another triumphant convoy.

The sun shining brightly; the waves gently tossing,
A playfully buffeting breeze.
Like straight driven shafts, latent on the crossing,
We follow our course through the seas.

We've only contempt for the foe we are braving;
And though we may never return,
We know that our flag will never stop waving
As they to their sorrow will learn.

A convoy of ships on the wide blue expanses
Where others have gone on before,
And every new convoy decreases the chances
Of those who have started the war.

THE ANGUAR CAMPAIGN

ANGUAR is the southernmost island in the Palau Islands Group, and its campaign was labeled Project Stalemate II (codename "Blue") for the PHILIPPINE LIBERATION.

Earl Shaffer left Hawaii around the first of August 1944 on a support troopship, *Sea Sturgeon*, **for a rendezvous in the South Pacific. The Battle for Anguar began on September 11 with bombardments by the** *USS Tennessee*, **a battleship, and dive bombers from the aircraft carrier** *USS Wasp*. **The Infantry and Marines landed September 17, 1944.**

TO DAD IF I DON'T COME THROUGH

The gray clouds are hanging low, Dad,
Close by the rail of the transport
Fringing a single lonely star
That shines through the gloomy grayness.
Somehow I feel as lonesome
At watching that far horizon
Long after the sunset fades
And billowing storm clouds gather
To the first white flicks of lightning;

As wild as the slate gray wild geese
That pass in the shadowed twilight
Like battle-bound plane formations.
It's wildness that's made of pathos
Deep burdened with nameless longing,
An unexplainable yearning
That makes me supremely lonely.
And now as this bleak horizon
Blurs out in a haze of memory,
I hear the humming of june bugs
And the chorus in the meadow
Of the silver voiced marsh peepers,
And the deep voiced frogs' marumphing,
And the squawk of the blue herons--
Friendly, yet wild, and as poignant
As the swelling of my heart.

Sometimes, when the mood possesses me,
Comes the thought with crystal clearness
That I really am a poet
And will always be as lonely
As the gray sky in the night.
The eyes of your children's children
Shall gaze from the old gray homestead
On out to the west horizon.
But deep in my heart is knowledge
That those kiddies won't be mine.
I'm lone as the mountain pathways
That my memories entwine.

A SOLDIER'S CREED

I never shall fear to meet the foe
In the air, on land or sea;
For any place I may chance to,
My GOD will be there with me.

He will be my guide and perfect shield
That can turn the sharpest sword.
He will give me faith that cannot yield
Though arrayed against a horde.

It is His to choose my span of life
And the way that I must die.
And though the horrors of war run rife,
'll know He is standing by.

And if by His will I come to fall,
It shall be no death for me
But passage over a prison wall
To life in Eternity.

VOYAGE TO ANGUAR

These pages contain the story
Of the troopship called **Sea Sturgeon**
With two thousand troops aboard her
On that long and varied journey
From the island base of Oahu
To the mandate Isle of Anguar
In the Palau group of islands.

It's an exciting story
For it's only service forces
Not the bold tale of assault troops
As they storm the Jap held beaches--
Just the lives of common soldiers
With their petty joys and troubles
When they're crowded close together
On a troopship in a convoy,

And their thoughts and culminations
When they reach their destination
On a still contested island.
For forty-two days we traveled
Five thousand miles to the westward
To build and equip an airbase
For bombing the Philippines.

Through weeks and months of preparing--
From painstaking long range planning,
We gathered, grouped, and assembled
The tools and the men for warfare.
And then on a day appointed
When "dry run" trials had ended,
The vast array was assembled
To make up the needed convoy
To go on a task force mission.

We drove in the early morning
Down a three-lane highway,
Oahu highway,
With our grotesque packs upon us
As we huddled by our baggage.

The pineapple trucks were hauling
The symbol of tropic Oahu
In crates that are drab unpainted
And stained with the constant seepage
Of pineapples freshly gathered
By workers in drudge-like labors
And colorless ways commercial
That lacks all that way of romance
Those folks on the mainland cherish,
As part of the magic islands
We found no longer existing.
We know that old Hawaii
Is gone to the passing legend
And songs of plaintive beauty.

We entered the teeming harbor
And boarded the big gray troopship.
Carried our bags on our shoulders;
Staggered in line up the gangplank
And blindly followed directions.

The ships are steadily filling
With men and supplies unending
Till at last the ship is loaded
And prepares to leave the harbor.
The fire tug called **Yonaguska**
Towed us away from the mooring
And brought us free of the small loch.

Oahu was wreathed in her rain clouds
As the troopship ploughed the channel,
And planes were whizzing around her
As she stood for the open sea.
A perfect rainbow was flashing
Out on the mists to the seaward
Almost as though a promise
Of speedy and fair weather passage,

Or promise of deeper ignorance
When havoc will rain about us--
And war will be close and deadly.
Slim crash boats came skimming swiftly
As she caught the ocean rollers,
And out on the decks the crewmen
Waved luck and a brief farewell.
Still smooth on the quiet waters,
She starts on her way to convoy
To the slow swish of her prow wash
And the tremble of her screws.

High on the bridge are signal flags
Fluttering tight in the trade winds,
And nearby the signal blinker
With watchers up in the gun pits
As Thunderbolt planes come buzzing,
Scarcely clearing the mastheads.

Troops on the main deck are huddled
In small groups talking or gambling
Or lined up along the railing
Taking their last look at Oahu,
At least for a long, long time.

We take up our place in the convoy.
All the troopships wallow
Through the gun blue waters
With most of the men half seasick
And bloated with high sea misery,
Staring across the horizon
In wordless hour-long poses.

And evening comes as a shadow--
From out in the empty distance
Cloaking the sea world in darkness
That brings with it time for blackout.
But high in the austere heavens
The moon and the stars unnumbered
Gleam out in their endless brilliance
In spite of the world of shadows
Till dawn is a window curtain
Of clouds in a blaze of glory,

Sunbeams as ending the cloudbanks
To startle the misty sea.

We scatter around the troopship.
And then, when you've settled quiet
From hours of patient searching
In a place that's not too crowded,
Somewhere along the railing,
The call is for lifeboat practice.
So back we must go to quarters
Down through the narrow hatchways
To stand by our bunks with patience
Till "abandon ship" is ordered.

And we scramble back up topside
To assemble at our stations,
Crossing the deck at the double
And forming along the railing
Till the practice run is over.
And then once again comes the twilight
And again the sweeping shadows,
And a violin well-mastered
In the classic vein of music
Like humoresque and "Blue Danube."
Wiegenlied and La Palma
Bring a touch ethereal
To the gray and silver shadows.

Sea Sturgeon

Photo Courtesy National History Center

We wrap in our OD blankets
To sleep out under the night sky,
Sprawling around on the main deck
Because of the crowded staleness
Of the quarters down below.
And so through the lights and shadows
The days and nights of passage,
The **Sea Sturgeon** steams onward
Carrying men and equipment
Outward and ever onward.

Today the Lieutenant assembled
Our crew for an early briefing--
No details, just meager outlines
Of plans for our installation.
We'll set up the mobile units
And then standby for equipment
To put in the final setup.

Later we heard an announcement
Over the loudspeaker system.
It said the first stop is the Marshalls
And Kwajalein is the island--
And so on through perfect weather
Up on the deck of the **Sea Sturgeon**,
Under the shade of a life raft:
Watching the foam of the prow wash
And the blueness of the sea,
Reading the **Reader's Digest**
Of the Normandy Invasion,
Living those days of battle
In vivid imagination.

The years on the lonely islands
Have brought me a sort of numbness
That separates mind and body
And renders me reconciled.
And now in the hush of the evening
A sonnet that's hectic written
By light of a moon cloud-hazy
That lights up a scene so austere
That only one may witness
Who wanders the wide blue desert;
Light hungry because of blackout,
And ponder for hours unspoken
The whims of the muted silence.

Soft through the night on the moonray water
Churning unchecked through the quiet sea
Bold with the vagrance of Gypsy hauteur--
Heartbroken strains of wild melody,
Silhouettes grouped in a life raft's shadow
Outcasts to whom the esthetic clings,
Wholly forgetful of looming battle,
Losing themselves in the livened strings.
Gray is the night as the lean, gray transport
Outward and onward toward the fight
Breasting the waves of the wide blue ramps.

The moon is low at midnight
And trailing across the water,
Trailing a pageant of glory
That brings incongruous whispers
Out of the memory shadows
Of somewhere we once called home.
We sail on a task force mission
On the maiden ship **Sea Sturgeon**
And out on her deck at midnight
Our thoughts are of many things.

Dawn is our own buoyant welcome,
Painting the calm sea with silver.
And now a touch of a rainbow
Clings to a cloud to the northward.
Swathed figures sprawl on the steel deck
Wrapped in their blankets and ponchos,
Stirring when reveille sounded--
Now trying to go back to sleep.

Soon we will be in the Marshalls.
Think there's a buddy of mine there
Back from the battle of Saipan,
Back with a wound in the shoulder.
Maybe I'll manage to see him,
Haven't seen him for three years.
What hopes we pin on an off chance;

Hopes that we know are hopeless.
Air raid sounded this afternoon,
An unidentified aircraft.
Everyone scurried below deck
Till abandon ship was sounded.
And we scrambled back up topside
And there the speaker informed us
That two Jap bases are nearby
And we are passing between them.
Everyone stood very quiet,
Not even the slightest murmur.

Last night the whole sky was empty
Except for the silver white moon.
But signs by day had been warning
And late in the quiet of midnight,
A squall caught the quiet **Sea Sturgeon**.
Those on deck got a soaking,
Drenching their bedrolls and clothing,
Before they could gain the hatchway.
But minutes later the moon shone
Brighter and clearer than ever--
Lonely, austere, and brilliant;
Then set in a hush before sunrise.

Our welcome to Kwajalein Atoll
Was rain in a wild wet storming
Just as we ploughed up the channel--
Clearing the deck of the troopship,
Chasing wet men to their quarters.

All through the hours of the morning
We crossed the world's largest atoll,
Eighty long miles to the anchorage,
Past hundreds of reef strung islets.
Men stood in swarms by the railing
Still not quite really believing
That this is mighty Kwajalein,
The king of the low atolls

Once more in the night a night rainstorm
Clearing the deck of the vessel,
Lashing in anger and fury
Behind the men in the hatchways;
And now from the curtain of night
The sun bursts from clouds of bondage
To gleam on the blue lagoon.

Got underway by afternoon
And stood out to sea at sundown,
Shipshape and formed in convoy
For the next lap of our journey.
And now the lights become sultry
And lightning flicks in the darkness
Which comes with the wan of the moon.
Day after day as we travel
The sea is calm and unruffled,
But gradually wakens and murmurs
Low on the prow of the troopship,
Whispering harshly and roughly.

Last night we heard a short lecture
As more or less of a briefing
To tell the men of the island,
And what we can be expecting
Because of the many diseases
They think the island harbors.

We sail for the island Anguar,
One of the Philippine outposts
In the Palau group of islands.
The men don't seem to be worried.
They're laughing, gambling and kidding,
Reading, talking, and sleeping.
They've learned to avoid much thinking
By day and among companions.
But what of the wide-eyed wakeness
That comes with the darkness?

Morale is at highest level.
The chow is more than expected.
The ship is capably handled.
We must have a first class skipper
In spite of those buzz saw orders.
The men seem vastly more cheerful
Which probably means the knowledge--
At last we're done with the waiting--
Out beyond the horizon
The fight has already started.
Today there were two more lectures
Of souvenir rules and restrictions,
And how we must treat the natives.

Church lasted an hour this morning.
The Chaplain gave us a sermon
On how we fight not for vengeance
And not against individuals
But really against the forces
That always have fought for chaos.
And so we should see foemen
As men who are tools of evil
And thus to be really pitied.
We must try in the future,
After the fighting is over,
To nullify cause for warfare
By treating men straight and fairly
As Jesus has always taught us.

And soon tempo has altered.
The island is getting nearer.
And now when we hear the ship's bell,
We know it isn't practice
But sweating some sort of danger,
Most likely a submarine.
We go to abandon ship stations
In the dark of the early morning
And stay there till after sunrise.

And nights become long and hectic
For those who defy the weather
By sleeping up on the hatches:
Wind and gray clouds and the patter
Of rain that constantly threatens
To fall in cold slashing torrents.
And one day the promise fulfilled,
Gray fog bounds the curved horizon
And grayness crept into our minds.

And then almost unexpected
Another stop in our journey--
A base we've had but a few months
And yet it's vastly important
As rendezvous for a task force.
Its spacious harbor is holding
A vast and varied armada
Of dozens and scores and hundreds
Of ships of every description--
Carriers, transports, destroyers
Gathered in one ample harbor
Far as the eye can encounter,
Countless and loaded and ready.
A force that is overwhelming.
So huge that it cannot falter;
So strong that it cannot fail.

And now as the shadows lengthen,
The sky is ablaze with sunset.
Red sky at night, says the sailor,
Means sunny skies on the morrow.
And now every doubt has vanished.
We know that our task force mission
Is destined to be accomplished.
The vast armada is ready,
And soon we sail for the sunset
To search for the rising sun.

The ways of a troopship are hard.
There's nothing about it gentle.
Everything's made out of tough steel
And jutting at crazy angles.

You bump into things in nighttime
And find they are very solid.
Your bunk is of steel pipe framework
With a canvas laced within it.
The bulkheads are walls of sheet steel;
The doors are shaped out of sheet metal
And all of the steel is welded.
Even the hinges are welded
With never a sign of a rivet
For that is the modern method.
The method that's fast and easy.

The days have been passing along--
Sweating the lineup at chow call,
Watching the fellows play poker.
And once when the ship's bell sounded,
The buzz saw voice of the speaker
Called the men to their stations
Sounding so serious and vibrant
That our scalps began to tingle.
And we thought it was the real thing
Till the same voice explained it
As another air raid practice.

And still we lay in the harbor
Without even having shore leave
Though nearby we see white beaches
That look cool and good for swimming.
We've never left the troopship
Since we boarded her at Oahu.
We huddle on deck and swelter
And hope for another rainstorm
To cool off the atmosphere.

We hear the news every morning:
Our target is being softened
By shore based and naval aircraft
And sometimes by naval shelling.
The next few days should bring D-day
Though nobody knows for certain,
And everyone's getting impatient
Wanting to get it over.

There have been a few small squabbles
For petty and baseless reasons,
But still it's been very quiet
For a group of men so crowded
In a space that scarcely holds them.
At last they let us have shore leave--
Three hours on a small side island.
Three times already assembled,
And every time it was canceled.

We went ashore on the fourth day.
Packed like sardines on a tank barge,
We stepped ashore on a white beach.
Took a short swim and then drifted
Talking to men on the island,
Curious and restless as always,
Then back to the ship at evening.
The next day we weighed up anchor
And formed in the outbound convoy.
And now is the time we've sweated.
Nothing now lies before us
But ocean and hostile beaches.

Anguar Beach

The ship is getting a scrubbing--
The quarters and decks and bulkheads
With soap and a lye solution.
The gunners are getting practice
By firing at plane drawn targets.
While all the ships of the convoy
Are blue gray dots on the water
Splashing up foam as they flounder
On through the dangerous waters.

Then late at night--general quarters--
And out we go through the hatchways
Fast as we can, though still careful,
Out through the tight blackout curtains,
Out to the darkness of the new moon
And tense expectant alertness.
A laugh almost hysterical
Sounds somewhere in the darkness
And only the barest murmur
Of low voiced talking succeeds it.
Thinking of home and of action,
Nobody outwardly nervous,
Though darkness hides all the faces
And only silhouettes bump you
To show you are not alone.
It might have been minutes or hours
We waited there in the darkness
Before the all clear was sounded,
And we could go back to our blankets.

Today we are staying topside.
The plans have suddenly altered.
Delay seems to be in the offing.
Our island has not been hit yet
And we must stand by for orders.
Somewhere not far from the island
In constant danger of air raids
And prowling submarines,
We're part of a landing action.

And yet we know almost nothing,
And all we can do is keep waiting.
Our gear is packed in our A bags;
Our bedrolls lashed on our field packs,
Ready to scramble when ordered.

Today we spotted the islands,
Hazy gray shapes on the portside,
And later sighted another
But this time over to starboard.
Carrier planes are patrolling,
Giving us fighter protection.
We rose in the dark this morning--
Went to abandon ship stations
To wait out the hour of dawning
When submarine danger is worst.
Nobody grumbled at waiting,
And no one had much to say.

We skirted around the island
And anchored off shore in convoy
In a reef enclosed lagoon.
Battleships, cruisers, and escorts
Gathered in groups at a distance.
Nearby, a mine has exploded,
Touched off by a round of gunfire;
And here we stand by for orders,
Alerted in dark of the evening.
But it was one of our planes,
And soon the all clear was sounded.

Then night and a watchful silence,
And the flickering of gunfire
Out along the southern horizon
Like the play of Northern Lights
And dawn is a fan uplifted--
Long streamers of tasseled sunshine
Over the low battle cruisers.

And so days passed while we waited,
And Tokyo Rose kept saying
That Japanese planes had bombed us
And had sunk the entire convoy.
Last night the sunset was different.
An ominous leaden blackness
Lay in the midst of the sunset.
It seemed a symbol of vagrance
As though we would be moving.

Today we have received orders--
We've moved from the off shore anchorage.
We've followed the group of islands
And stopped to the south of Anguar.
The baggage is packed and piled;
The packs are secure and ready.
Everything's hustle and bustle,
Hurried but systematic.
Soon we'll be heading shoreward
Long past the time we were scheduled--
The Japs have been causing trouble.

How can men wait so offhanded
Reading a novel or Western,
A **Time** or a **Reader's Digest**,
Ignoring the rumble of gunfire
Rolling across the water?

The Japs seem to still be fighting
Even on tiny Anguar.
We hear the news on the speaker
That comes from the states on short wave.
The news takes a long, long detour
Before we learn what we're doing.

That night we lay between Anguar
And the island of Peleliu,
Not anchored, but scarcely moving
And waiting the coming of sunrise.
Star shells are blooming on Anguar,
Most likely to hinder snipers.

On Peleliu is a display
Like the Fourth of July celebration
With sporadic bursts of tracers
As though at a strafing airplane.
The whump of heavy artillery
Rolls out across the water,
Scarcely heard through the rumble
And grunt of the troopship's motor.
Far into the night the star shells
Still blossom beneath the rain clouds,
And still at dawn it's raining.
The water is rough for barges;
And surf is pounding on Anguar.
The sea is heaving and tossing
And debarkation is canceled.

But still no signs of abating--
By the middle of the afternoon
We circled around the island
Searching for smoother waters.
Then over we go, regardless,
Down to the barge on a rope net.

Hold the net taunt for the others
While the barge lifts up and lowers
To the surge of the angry rollers.
But she finally is loaded
And without a serious mishap.
And the coxswain turns her shoreward
Through the slapping, slashing water--
Slopping water through the front ramp
As we peer out through the grating.

Then we round a tiny headland
On the foam crest of a breaker
Through a wreckage bordered channel
To a sort of makeshift mooring.
And we scrambled quickly over
To the rocky shore of Anguar.

All about us are the wreckage
And the salvage parts of barges
That have not survived the grueling,
Costly grind of cargo handling.
For the coral shores of Anguar
Are as savage and as senseless
As a mad dog wild with hunger.

We proceed to our campsite
Where had been the village Saipan
But was now ghastly rubble
For the Japs had used foundations
And the masonry as barriers
And had dug their caves and foxholes
In amongst the village houses.
So the rampaging artillery
Leveled all in one vast carnage,
And we pick among the rubble
For a place to pitch a pup tent
And watch all the while for snipers.
In the midnight, rain came lashing--
Just the first of many showers
On the tropic Isle of Anguar

So we found our mobile units
And set up communications.
The next night found us huddled
Unprotected by our shelters
While the anti-aircraft blazoned
In a wild display of action
At a plane that dodged above us
In and out of moonlit cloudbanks.
Till at last he left and quiet
Settled back across the island.
Gradually we cleared the campsite,
And a kitchen shack was set up
Though we still ate field type rations
And were nearly always hungry.

Day by day the time is passing
In a tense and watchful waiting
For the Japs still hold positions
In the rocks and mines and caves
Of the northwest hills of Anguar
Where a single hidden sniper
Can delay a whole division.
Flares are endlessly exploding
As the Japs keep infiltrating,
And we've built defense positions
Should a *Banzai* charge develop.

Japs are slipping through the frontlines
In ever increasing numbers
And have started sniper fighting,
Shooting a guard or an MP
From the cover of the jungle.
They are silent and quick as shadows
And we're posting double guards now.
We have lost more men in mop-ups
Than were lost in actual fighting.

Japanese Cave on Anguar

And there are still little pockets
Where the Japs are still defiant.
So we carry loaded rifles,
And we sleep with them beside us.
The flares are always floating
In the darkness of the night sky
While we lay with loaded weapons
In our lonely army blankets.

And our sleep is never slumber
But the restlessness of tension,
Or we crouch in guard positions
With our fingers to the trigger
And our eyes fixed on the jungle
Watching by light of the star shells
For the slightest hostile action.

We hear lots of random firing,
And the almost daily stories
Of the grim sporadic fighting.
One dawn there was heavy firing--
Lots of bullets ricocheting
From a nearby bivouac area.
And we got the story later
Of a Jap who had infiltrated
And had wounded several soldiers
In the first dim light of morning.
And then when he had been wounded,
He killed himself with his last grenade.

And of how the weather squadron
Had a wild close quarter melee
When a Jap got in their quarters
And killed himself and an officer
And wounded most of the squadron.
Now there is no more fighting
Except lone and futile snipers
Killed occasionally at outposts.
And the caves have all been captured
In the crevassed north shore boulders.

The airport's in operation
And that was the main objective.
The ragged Isle of Anguar
Has been cleared of rocks and jungle
For the camps and installations;
And the roar of heavy bombers
Punctuates the nightly silence.

So the trek and job is ended--
Run its course and expended.
And the trail seems long and fleeting
Back through other operations
On toward the unknown future.
And now in the dead of the night,
The island is wrapped in the glow
Of stars that are shining brightly.
A tense and inscrutable peace
Lies on the brow of tomorrow.
And over the flash of the breakers
That heave and pound the shoreline,
Thought flees from the island Anguar
To other and farther places.

MISERY PERSONIFIED ON ANGUAR

Forty long days of voyaging
Across the tropic sea
Most of the way not knowing
Where the landing would be.

"Island Secured in 3 Days"
The gleeful headline cries.
The facts speak otherwise:
Six weeks and all day long
Crouched in a makeshift slit trench;
Far in the dead of night
Sickened by reeking death stench,
Straining hearing and sight;
Rifle loaded and ready
Cradled across lap;
Gripping a grim Machete
And watching for a Jap.

ANGUAR MOON

Somewhere the sun is shining
But not on Anguar Isle
Where homesick men are pining
In GI army ctylo.

Somewhere the food is tasty
And water fresh and cold,
Where mud is not so pasty
And bombers aren't so bold.

Somewhere young people marry
And lovesick lovers croon,
But not where snipers tarry
Beneath a tropic moon.

Somewhere are peace and minstrels
Where people dare to stroll;
And not bright flaring star shells
And guards crouched in a hole.

Somewhere to live is pleasure
And friendly people smile,
Where kindness metes its measure,
But not on Anguar Isle.

OUT OF THE LINE

All covered with dust, thick caked with sweat
In a grimy streaked mantle,
They're marching along the dusty road
Away from a jungle battle
They've blasted the Japs from limestone caves
Up north in the jumbled boulders.
They've buried buddies in white marked graves,
And they march with drooping shoulders.

Their whiskers are long; their clothes are limp
And hanging like wrinkled sacking.
And here they come plodding down the road
In shoes that are torn and cracking.

They're not such a very pretty sight
As they come away from battle--
Down the rutted road in ragged clothes
And a grimy, gray-white mantle.

Romauldo Hill was a series of coral ridges or boulders in the northwest corner of Anguar Island. The Japanese had dug labyrinths and caves inside the coral ridges. It took the soldiers more than four weeks of using flame-throwers, grenades, demolition charges, and hand to hand combat to extinguish Japanese resistance in that area of the island. Finally, the Americans bulldozed ground to cover the openings to the caves. nn

ANGUAR CEMETERY

There's a little gray stone chapel
With a low stone wall around
On a bit of Anguar Island
That is truly hallowed ground.
For the rows of snow white markers
Neatly spaced within that wall
Mark the men who died for freedom
For themselves and for us all.

They would not have chosen Anguar
As the place where they would lie
And but few would have admitted
That their time had come to die.

For of death remains unspoken
What is thought but never said,
And we never reck too closely
Of the next potential dead.

There are many other graveyards
On the island battlegrounds
Where the star of David mingles
And the plain white cross abounds,

Where they rest who once were vested
With the strife of flesh and bone
And have paid the price unstinted
For your freedom and their own.

There's a little cemetery
Where our fallen buddies lie.
And the island was not worth it
That so many men must die,

If they hadn't fought and fallen
For an island stepping stone
That has vast strategic value,
Though no value of its own.

CLAIMING THE NIGHT

There's a clamor of wild commotion
In the first three graders hut:
It's eve of an Anguar Christmas
And the guys here celebrate.
It's not that they're so contented
But they've sampled of the cup
And they've lost their inhibitions
At a most alarming rate.

The radio's blaring loudly
And the addled voices rise
In song and a wild confusion
To augment the strident blare.
Out in the night are moon clouds
That sail in the lofty skies,
The beautiful tasmal offering
Of a loveliness to spare.
The essence of contradiction
Of carousal and delight,
The flare of complete abasement
And the calm uplifting peace,
Which shall remain unhindered
To wholly claim the night?
The sky for its patient beauty
Lives on though riots cease.

LONG AFTER THE BATTLE

There's a tattered old red bunting
At the end of the telephone line
On a jagged old gray boulder
That juts out over the water
On the wild north shore of Anguar.

A storm has shrouded Peleliu,
Completely blotting it from view;
And yet the sun is still shining here.
West, south, and east the sky is clear.

Foam blankets the reef-choked shoreline
In picturesque snow white mantle
Where once was the hawk-eyed vigil
And the grim staccato battle.

SHATTERED SHORE

Boulders lay in rank confusion
With the torn look of debris:
Battered boards and old shell cases
And the worn trunk of a tree;

Anguar rocky beach

Tattered clothes and rusty weapons
Anguar's Blue Beach
In a weather-beaten pile
That extends on Anguar's "blue beach"
For at least a half a mile.

Just a small scale shore invasion,
Just a flank-attack is all--
As a trifling indication
Of what makes a fortress fall:

Just a skirmish in a battle,
Or a footnote on a page
Like an insect crushed in passage
By a bull moose on the rage.

Yes, and even all of Anguar
Was a small dim scale event
In the holocaust of carnage
In which countless lives are spent.

And these trees, torn short by gunfire,
Are but remnants of it all
Though it took a savage pounding
Just for small Anguar to fall.

ANGUAR SWAN SONG

Sure there's cause for high rejoicin'
And no reason for dismay,
And our winged thoughts have dreams
Of home adornin'
For the Radio Construction
Got the welcome news today
That we're leavin' Anguar island
In the mornin'.

Sure our eyes are shinin' brighter
And we're packin' up our stuff
To begin the trip across the briny ocean.
And our hearts could not be lighter
Nor the time be short enough
To be puttin' travel orders Into motion.

And we cast a look of longing
For the northeast sky at dawn
And the long trail's new beginning
In the gloaming.
When you wake up in the morning,
We have hopes that we'll be gone
For the Radio Construction men
Are homing.

Sure our feet are in a panic
And we're feelin' far from blue.
And for us it's not occasion
For forlorning
For we got the news today,
And we'll say farewell to you
When we leave from Anguar island
In the morning.

ANGUAR GOODBYE

Goodbye, little coral island
Where our buddies fought and died.
Goodbye, for the time has fallen
When our hopes are not denied.
The call of command is stronger
Than the men who would restrain.
We dwell on your rocks no longer
And we never will again.

The wings of the sky road beckon
And we're taking to the sky.
It's hail and farewell, I reckon,
And there's none gladder than I.

LONE BRAVE'S VOYAGE

Lone Brave rides the barren waters
From beyond the borderline
In his heart is welling laughter
And his bleak eyes start to shine.

In his heart new hopes are soaring
And his thoughts are homeward bound,
For he soon will be exploring
On his old stomping ground.

Three years and a score of islands
Out over the far-flung sea,
The palm and the eucalyptus
And the gray niaouli tree.

The glare of the blinding coral
And the tangled jungle vines,
Where the joy of life is frugal
Away from the shining pines.

Lone Brave yields his humble yearning,
And the dawn breaks into morn
On the day of his returning
To the land where he was born.

Dawn in the South Pacific

Earl and Walter first met about the center of this picture at age 5.
Photo Courtesy Shaffer Family

WALTER WINEMILLER

Walter on furlough prior to Iwo Jima campaign
Photo courtesy the Shaffer family taken at the Shaffer home

BALLAD OF WALTER

We were five years old when we met at the boundary line
Where Fox Run turns against the trees and the willow thicket twine.
He was tow haired with sky blue eyes while mine were black and gray.
It seemed we always had been friends and it always was that way.

Just neighbor kids down through the years to the age of twenty-two--
The barefoot walks, the fishing trips, and the harvest working crew.
Chasing the polecats on the meadow wide under the full harvest moon,
Then I write and tell you some more to make you swoon:

On Anguar Island at the break of day I wake to a sudden dread.
Marines landed on Iwo at dawn and I know that Walter is dead.
Scout sniper platoon caught on the beach, the burst of a mortar shell.
What does the ballad of Walter teach: That war is certainly hell.

ON IWO JIMA

Over the water northward
The Fourth and Fifth Marines
Were landing on Iwo Jima.
In my hand I hold a letter
Written aboard ship by Walter
At the convoy rendezvous.
My soul was sick with knowledge
That Walter was already dead
Or dying on the beachhead.

Again, a few days later
Came a telegram from home.
Hail and farewell, Trail Partner,
No more could a warrior do
Than die on Iwo Jima.

Cablegram sent to Earl by Evan confirming Walter's death.
Photo Courtesy Evan Shaffer

TO WALTER

Breeze of the moonlit meadows
Sigh through the pines again--
Follow the trails we wended
Rustle each lonely glen.

Whisper for me a message
In night trail monotone.
Give him a fond "Aloha"
From Lone Brave all alone.
Soft is the sigh of the pine trees.
Here we have palms instead.
Softly they sway and murmur;
Here's what they softly said,
"Me-le-Ka-li-ki-ma-ka"
Many returns of the day--
Greetings from out of the sunset,
"Aloha" from far away.

SOUTH OF THE SUNSET

Dedicated to Walter Winemiller and
William Winemiller, Jr.

South of the sunset
Were wild waves rolling
Crashing on coral
And war bells tolling
Gunfire and bombast

And lonely vigil
On out-of-way atolls
With sea birds crying
And young men dying.

South of the sunset were wild waves dancing,
Sometimes repelling, sometimes entrancing;
South of the sunset, tall palms sighing
On atoll islands and sea birds flying.

South of the sunset: hurricanes howling
On monsoon waters, and gay ships prowling.
South of the sunset: a pearl moon shining
And men who marveled but still were pining.

Walter Winemiller and his younger brother William Winemiller, Jr. were in the same United States Marine Division. They both stormed the volcanic ash beaches of Iwo Jima on February 19, 1945. Word reached William, Jr. (or Gord) on the first day of the battle that his brother Walter and his brother's entire scout sniper platoon had been re-grouping after the beach assault in a bomb crater when they were struck by a hand thrown grenade. Junior went to the bomb crater and identified his brother's body. Walter Winemiller is buried in The National Military Cemetery in Honolulu. While "souvenir hunting" at night (for Japanese *Banzai* attackers), Junior suffered severe injuries. After his return from the Anguar Campaign to his homebase in Oahu, Earl Shaffer visited Junior Winemiller in the hospital. nn

William Winemiller, Jr.
Photo Courtesy Shaffer Family

BIGGEST KILL

After Iwo, the young marine
In sick bay for his wound to heal
Spoke somberly of battle days
To one who was a life long friend.
"One night I heard a stealthy noise
Out in the darkness somewhere near.
So close I could not even check the other guards.
What should I do?

"The orders were: no one should move
Or make a noise so this must be
The enemy. I pulled the pin
From one grenade; tossed it and yelled,
'Fire in the hold!' and hit the deck;
Then tossed another after it.
So close it was that I had feared
Shrapnel would hit the other guards.
We looked by daylight and we saw
A pile of Japs around a gun.

"We used flame-throwers on a cave
One day and thought no one could live
Through it, but when we turned away
One came headlong with bayonet.
My back was turned; somebody yelled.
I couldn't move; I'd have been killed
But someone's rifle blazed away.
The Jap fell sprawling at my feet.

"Got hit on Iwo at the last.
Was on a hunt for souvenirs,
Walking along a jungle path.
A rifle shot. The bullet fanned
My cheek. I hit the deck but then
Knew that I must keep on the move.
I heard a bolt click, then a shot.
The bullet cut my shoulder strap.

"Guessed where he was by then and dove
Toward him, but the next shot caught
Me near my collarbone and down
I went thinking this is the end.
Woke up on a hospital ship
Two days later and here I am."

My father Evan Shaffer told me the rest of this story: When the Japanese soldier jumped from his cover to finish off Junior Winemiller, a barrage of bullets hit him from several Marine guns. nn

LONE BRAVE'S DEDICATION

These are the writings of Lone Brave
Who dreams when the lights are low
Of the Allegheny Mountains
And the fur trails in the snow.

Lone Brave is sad when he's dreaming
Of those carefree days of yore
For his trailmate fell on Iwo
And will roam the trail no more.

From left to right : Gord, Walter Winemiller, Evan and Earl Shaffer (Note Walter's skunk skin hat.)
Photo Courtest Shaffer Family

Where are you now, Compadre,
Are there trails where you have gone?
Are the mornings crisp and frosty
In the land beyond the dawn?

Do you draw a bow as deftly
And do game and fur abound?
And does snow fall just as thickly
On the Happy Hunting Ground?

LONE BRAVE'S FANTASY

As Lone Brave sits in reverie
When the fire is burning low,
The flames forge out a phantasy
From out of the long ago.

For Lone Brave senses far and clear
The dream of a passing day
When war was just a ghastly sere
And the youth must go away.

The Chinook grass was touched with green
And the birds were headed north.
The air was warm and crisp and clean
When the warrior ventured forth.

The oak leaves promised early corn
And a gray dawn filled the sky--
The day the chieftain vowed with scorn
That the tribal foes must die.

With bow and well filled quiver slung
And provision pouch by side,
Tireless of feet and stout of lung,
They struck for the range divide.

The warpath led for many miles
And the haughty chieftain led;
But lest the band succumb to wiles
They must send out scouts ahead.

The young and the quick of eye and limb
And intelligent of mien
Must haunt each ridge and canyon rim
And report what they had seen.

The keen alertness of the hawk
Must sharpen their youthful gaze
For out ahead the foemen stalk,
Preparing the ambuscade.

They came at last to hostile land
And the vanguard gave the sign;
And soon the gathered forces joined
In a hectic battle line.

And warriors far from home
Found a last grim resting place
With tears of grief as yet to come
To many a loved one's face.

For war is ever fain to lay
The best and the strongest low;
And even then as now today
It's the chosen who must go.

The ones who forge out far ahead
Where only the boldest strive,
Are often among the dead
When the rest return alive.

And Lone Brave sees a warrior there
Who lies in a grave of sand,
A warrior with yellow hair
Afar in a stranger land.

And Lone Brave pleads that all may see
The truth of the cause of war
And watch and pray by night and day
That the plagues may come no more.

LONE BRAVE'S RETURN

You gave me the name of Lone Brave
    When the trails led out to war.
    For you there is no returning
    To the trails we knew before.

    There it's never really silent
    For the songs of many birds,
But there's wondrous peace and quiet
    Far beyond expressive words.

I've come to the old trails, Walter,
    In the full of harvest time
When the warmth of Indian Summer
    Brings the earth to fullest prime.

    A duck flew up in the woodland
    And a pheasant on the hill.
    The corn is ripe on the farmlands,
    And the old war guns are still.

    The first of the leaves have fallen
    From the shag bark hickory trees,
    And there's just a touch of winter
    In the early morning breeze.

Lone Brave is your Trailmate, Walter,
    Till the last lone trail be found;
    And his step will never falter
    To the Happy Hunting Ground.

TRAIL BUDDY PARDNER

    Sit up a little closer, Pal,
    The fire is burnin' low.
    The coals are faintly glowin
    And clean dry bundles blaze.
    We'll snag a couple extras
    Though it's almost time to go
    And talk of old time pow wows
Thru' the drifting wood smoke haze.
    Remember that fire kindled
    Every year at harvest time

As sort of a ceremony
When we roasted tender corn
And spoke of the full abundance
That reaper finds so prime
From earliest golden wheat fields
Till the autumn frosts are born?
Remember that little campfire
By the stream called Conocochegue
That lies in the long wide valley
Of the Tuscarora range,
And those short excursions
That we took most every week
Just to ramble of a Sunday
Year by year without a change?
And maybe you weren't in person,
But your spirit still was there,
When a lonely campfire blazoned
In the brushlands of Caroline,
When we went on war maneuvers
In the late fall of the year
Through the scattered hills and valleys
And the groves of long leaf pine.
And down on a little island
In the far off Coral Sea
When we gathered round a bonfire
Underneath the Southern Cross,
We sang the old-time folksongs,
A guy named Tex and me.
And it kinda stirred my memory
To a poignant sense of loss.
Those are fires that always linger
In the forefront of the flame
Though red firelight always flickers
In that special sort of way;
And it gives a guy a feeling
That he can't quite give a name.
It's the same dim half lost feeling
That is in my mind today.

REGRETFUL TRAILS

There's a silver moon on the fields tonight
And the dew is wet on my huntin' shoes;
But there's someone gone and it isn't right
And the charm is lost from the moonlit views.
There's a moon hung high in a cloudless sky.
There the streams run clear in the same old way,
And my thoughts return to the days gone by
When we roamed unhindered by night or day.
But the fields are haunted by memories
Of the trailmate lost on the fields of war
And the night wind lurks in the forest trees.
But it's not the same as it was before.
And I sing no song to the wildling breeze
For my pardner died in the Southern Seas.

Walter Winemiller
Photo Courtesy Shaffer Family

One of Earl's Crews

Earl with bow

REQUIEM

VETERAN'S MOON SONNET
You're shining so full yet there's no need to fear.
No bombers are coming; no foxhole is near.
I'm far from the place where the night vultures prey,
Yet somehow I long for the coming of day.
Pearl Moon, am I dreaming or can this be true
That I can be standing here looking at you
And need not be crouching for hours in a hole
While wishing you banished with body and soul?
Oh, Moon, shall I ever be able to gaze
With untroubled calm on your brilliant rays
And find in you romance and beauty and life
Instead of these hauntings of horror and strife?
I fear that I never can find you again
As guiltless and lovely and carefree as then.

TOO MANY MEMORIES

When the stars are tinkling sleighbells
In a land untouched by snow
And the waves are rippling spangles
In the moonlight's tropic glow,

When the vast globe girdling ocean
Turns its wrath away from men,
Memories and deep emotion
Touch our lonely hearts again.

The night seems filled with sentiment
And a vortex tantalized
With flashes of vast presentiment
In a chaos mesmerized.

I sense in the crowded blackness
A melody dimly heard,
And out of the brimming slackness
The scold of a Myna bird.

I see in a wide-eyed vision
The islands I used to know
And long, as a soul in prison,
For places I cannot go.

The gang by the fire on Belep
And the wee land-locked lagoon
Or watching a shadowed landscape
By the matchless Thio moon.

The ships in Noumea Harbor
Or the planes at Plains de Guy;
The deck of a sailing schooner
When the seas are running high.

The Hula on Tongareva
And the Fiji Tra-la-la;
The Native on Nanumea
And his farewell word "Tofa."

The starkness of Funafuti
Exposed by a bomber's moon
Or lashed by the wailing fury
Of a rampaging typhoon.

Six months on the wretched coral
Of the island called Anguar;
Five months on the barren Johnston
Where the sea birds gather far.

The squalor of Pango Pango
And the sea moon shining bright;
The crackle of distant gunfire
And the star shells in the night.

The feel of a lonely foxhole
In the darkness and the rain
When the *Banzai* boys are fretful
From the last ditch battle strain.

The hum of a transport's motors
Up along the trackless sky
Far above the ocean waters
And a cloud goes trailing by.

The ways of a crowded troopship
In a convoy outward bound
And the deadly palls of silence
After air raid warnings sound.

The fear that's a knot inside you
Up a ninety foot high pole,
And the way the sweat will blind you
When you dig a coral hole.

The way that the years go flitting
In an endless numbing haze
When there's never chance for quitting
And your mind becomes a maze.

And there is no thing called freedom,
And no choice but to remain
With the war that flouts all wisdom
And the thoughts you can't explain.

I hear the sigh of the South wind
As we lined the Southern Cross,
And our sorrow seems predestined
With a hopeless sense of loss.

The ghosts of the past come trailing
In a long nostalgic train.
And forgetfulness, in failing,
Brings them all to life again:

See the wild rock studded coastlines
Of a score of scattered isles;
See the brush bedraggled inclines
And the friendly native smiles;

Seeing pass in swift procession
The faces of men I knew
In vivid recollection
As the thoughts pass in review.

Recalling those old companions
Who shared what little they had;
The casual ones and the close ones
And my heart is full and sad.

All poignant and vivid memories,
Drawn so sharply and so clear
From the distant island barriers,
Gather slowly year by year.

From the war torn, sunbaked islands
And a vast array of men
Scattered and gone to the four winds,
Never to gather again.

Yet far in the fulsome bygone
Still glimmer the days of yore
That are free of all connection
With the vagaries of war.

The years of a carefree childhood,
As free as the whip-poor-wills,
That call in the twilight wildwood
Back home in the rolling hills.

Yes, the mind brings back the memories
In a vivid resume
Representing countless forays
That can never fade away.

As the stars in countless numbers
Pierce the deep night darkening blue,
So the pathos only slumbers
Till the twilight dawns anew.

DIRGE FOR THE DEAD

In the prime of youthful manhood,
In the dawning years of life,
They go to be slain and offered
To the devil gods of strife.

The best that the race can muster--
The choice of body and mind--
Are given up to slaughter
For gluttonous greed and pride.

The sires of our unborn children:
Our brothers, fathers, and sons
Are meat for the sateless cauldron
To feed the ravening guns.

The stigma of death and sorrow
Holds unremitting sway,
And only The Great Tomorrow
Can promise a better day.

TAPS

Haunting and poignant and lone--
Adrift on the still night air--
The tones of the bugle blown
Hint vaguely of despair.
Telling us one and all
That death is a minor thing--
That all must expect its call
And find it is naught to sting.

Taps at a soldier's bier
Or taps in the dead of night
Tell us we have no fear
But only to fight for right.

Earl's Final Resting Place
Photo Courtesy Shaffer Family

Old Glory in the South Pacific war zone

GLOSSARY

ailerons: either of two monster flaps on the wings of an airplane that can be used to control the plane's rolling and banking maneuvers
ambushcade: ambush
Anguar: the southernmost island in the Palau Islands group. There is more information about Anguar in the ANGUAR CAMPAIGN section.
annals: records of history; chronicles
Flanders: Flanders Fields is an American cemetery for doughboys in Belgium (World War I soldiers)
Banzai: Japanese war cry or cheer; a reckless and utterly ferocious military attack by the Japanese, usually at night on sleeping GI's
bale: a great evil or sorrow
Banshee wail: a shrill, terrified scream; In Irish folklore, "The Banshee of Ireland" is the most widely known Irish fairy tale second only to the Leprechaun. The Banshee usually appears in the form of a wailing woman who has the sound of a wailing owl at the coming of death. The *Banshee Wail* in the poem is the name of Pat Magee's plane. It probably made a sound similar to a screeching owl or the wailing woman in the folktale. "The Luck of the *Banshee's Wail*" is his own ballad about his airplane's escapades.
Big Ears: Earl's nickname for Walter
bivouac: a temporary military encampment
Bougainvillea: the largest island in the Solomon Islands where an important battle was fought to establish a refueling and supply base for Guadalcanal (today is spelled Bougainville)
caste: social favoritism
Chinook: An American Indian tribe in Oregon; usually refers to an unseasonably warm wind in coastal Oregon or the eastern Rocky Mountain slopes
constancy: steadfastness under duress
coterie: an exclusive group of persons with a unifying common interest or purpose
coxswain: the steersman sailor who has charge of a ship or boat, helmsman
crevasse: deep crack, crevice, or fissure in the earth
dissension: partisan and contentious, quarreling
doughboy: a World War I American soldier; Earl Shaffer called himself a doughboy because he was born on November 8, 1918, the day that the Germans stopped fighting in World War I.

doughfoot: infantry man in the US Army, especially in World War II, a blend of doughboy from World War I (doughfeet is plural or doughfoot is also a slang plural)
***Esprit de Corps*:** strong enthusiasm and devotion
fain: compelled
foe, foemen: the enemy (Japanese warriors)
gloam or gloaming: a canopy of twilight
grotesque: departing from the natural or expected, bizarre
guileless: guiltless
hauteur: haughtiness, arrogance
hep: military term for marching with spirit
Heroic Sonnet: 18 lines of poetry (an additional quatrain) with a special end rhyme pattern; the meter and rhythm is usually iambic pentameter
humoresque: a genre of romantic music characterized with fanciful humor and wit--example: Schumann's "Humorske in B flat major" and "Blue Danube"
Immelmann: A turn in which an airplane in flight completes half of a loop and then rolls half of a complete turn.
LaPalma: music indigenous to the Canary Islands and spread to California during World War II; an important strategic outpost in World War II and the music played a crucial role in Operation Torch
lay: spread out, resting on the surface (the armada in the harbor)
livened: lively
Lone Brave: Walter's nickname for Earl
lorn: desolate, forsaken, forlorn
Maitaki: There is no such island but some islands were abundant in maitake mushrooms
moldering, moldered: with mold, decaying and crumbling into small particles
Mother Hubbard (dresses): old fashioned European and full-length
Marshalls: the Marshall Islands in Micronesia
macaque: a short-tailed, soft haired monkey in southern Asia
Myna: a bird in Southern Asia
niaouli tree: gray-green leaves, melaleuca or Paper Bark Tea Tree
Nippons: Japanese
OD: olive drab, military issued blankets
Oligarchy: a government which is ruled by a small, corrupt group
pardner: slang for partner
petrel: any small long-winged seabird that flies far from land
phantasy: fantasy
play in hob: to work mischief

presentiment: premonition
reck: reckon, to worry or care about
rising sun: the Japanese have a rising sun on their flag
sateless: not satisfied or not satiated
scrappy: determined spirit
Sea Sturgeon: A standard C3 type freighter of civil registry
In 1944 she made her first and only round trip voyage from the West Coast to the Southern Pacific War Theater during July to December 1944.
sere: withered
shavetail bars: newly commissioned Second Lieutenant
sons of heaven: Japanese who worshiped the rising sun
souvenirs: nickname for Japanese soldiers--"souvenir hunting"
star shells: They are used at night to light up a battlefield and give off a glowing green light.
tasmal: "phantasmal"---unreal, illusory, spectral
tensile: capable of tension or stress
tome: a large unwritten book or large book
Tongareva: largest atoll in the Cook Islands
vagary: unpredictable, inconstant
vagrant, vagrance: no established residence, one who wanders; having no fixed course
vein: a distinctive mode of expression
Wiegenlied: German title of the original lullaby by J. Brahms, his "Cradle Song"
wildling: wild